THE SWEET & THE SOUR

Copyright © 1991 Omnibus Press
(A Division of Book Sales Limited)
Edited by Chris Charlesworth
Cover designed by Lisa Pettibone
Book designed by Lisa Pettibone & Monica Chrysostomou
Picture research by Paul Giblin
Typesetting & co-ordination by Caroline Watson

ISBN 0.7119.2075.3
Order No. OP 45632

All rights reserved. No part of this book may be reproduced in any form or by any electronic or mechanical means, including information storage or retrieval systems, without permission in writing from the publisher, except by a reviewer who may quote brief passages.

Exclusive distributors:

Book Sales Limited,
8/9 Frith Street,
London W1V 5TZ, UK.

Music Sales Corporation,
225 Park Avenue South,
New York, NY 10003, USA.

Music Sales Pty Ltd.,
120 Rothschild Avenue,
Rosebery, NSW 2018, Australia.

To the Music Trade only:
Music Sales Limited,
8/9 Frith Street,
London W1V 5TZ, UK.

Typeset by Saxon Printing Ltd, Derby, England
Printed in England by KPC Group, South Willesborough, Ashford, Kent.

Peter Anderson: 16/17, 36, 45(T&B), 48, 52, 54, 57, 60, 61, 64/5, 68, 79, 80(T&B), 89, 92.
Kobal Collection: 66, 67.
LFI: FC, 8, 10, 12, 13, 15, 19, 20(L&R), 21, 22, 24, 25(L&R), 26, 27, 33, 41, 46, 49, 56, 58, 59, 69, 72, 74, 76, 77, 83, 84, 85, 95, 96.
Pictorial Press: 9, 32(B), 44, 51.
Relay: 59(B).
Retna: 30, 32(T&L), 34, 35, 47, 55.
Starfile: 28, 29, 71.
Chris Taylor: 43, 91.

Every effort has been made to trace the copyright holders of the photographs in this book but one or two were unreachable. We would be grateful if the photographers concerned would contact us.

THE FINE YOUNG CANNIBALS' STORY

THE SWEET
&
THE SOUR

BRIAN EDGE

OMNIBUS PRESS
LONDON · NEW YORK · SYDNEY

ACKNOWLEDGEMENTS

The author would like to thank the following sources and their respective publications:
Isabel Appio, Kate Davies, Bruce Dessau, Liam Fay, Malu Halasa, Dean Haynes, Dave Henderson, Mike Hrano, Alan Jackson, Richard Jackson, Graham K., Richard Lowe, Stuart Maconie, Anna Martin, Steve Masters, Ted Mico, Mike Mitchell, Ro Newton, Betty Page, Deanne Pearson, Steve Pond, Ian Pye, Jaynie Senior, William Shaw, Jim Shelley, Paul Simper, Will Smith, Mat Snow, Mike Souter, Andy Strike, Karen Swayne, Adrian Thrills and Debbi Voller.

CONTENTS

FYC 1   **DESPERATELY SEEKING ROLAND**   9

FYC 2   **MAD ABOUT THE BOYS**   29

FYC 3   **SEX, GINSENG AND ROCK 'N' ROLL**   49

FYC 4   **LIONS AFTER SLUMBER**   69

       DISCOGRAPHY   93

FRONTISPIECE

Rub a dub-dub,
Three men in a tub,
And how do you think they got there?
The butcher, the baker,
The candlestick maker,
They all jumped out of a rotten potato,
'Twas enough to make a man stare.
                              Trad

INTRODUCTION

The Sweet & The Sour was originally planned as an 'official' book on Fine Young Cannibals, that is to say a book which benefited from the band's input and from which they would earn a royalty. As part of the agreement with Fine Young Cannibals, Omnibus Press would allow the band to vet the manuscript, make changes and assume some control of the design; in return we would get rare unseen pictures from their personal collections and, we hoped, an 'inside' story containing previously unpublished details and stories about their thoughts, words and deeds.

That, at least, was the spirit of the contract we entered into with Fine Young Cannibals in the summer of 1989.

Unfortunately this did not come to pass. Although author Brian Edge was allowed limited 'access' to Fine Young Cannibals, his manuscript was rejected by the band. They then offered to find an alternative author who would deliver a second manuscript within a matter of weeks. Several months passed and it became apparent that they had been unable to find an alternative author; neither were they particularly forthcoming about their reasons for rejecting the original manuscript, other than to state that in their opinion it was 'boring' and, in a roundabout way, suggest that it was not in keeping with their 'image', or the 'image' they wished to portray. Indeed, certain changes they requested before rejecting the manuscript outright involved the removal of references to their more human traits. These changes have been honoured.

The author is an old school friend of one of the band members. Both he and Omnibus Press felt the manuscript was eminently publishable, and when Fine Young Cannibals failed to produce the alternative manuscript they had promised we took the decision to publish the original manuscript rather than scrap the project. The result can be found between these covers.

DESPERATELY SEEKING ROLAND

A career in pop music, so they say, is about as long as a piece of string, and just as likely to become tatty at the tail end. Andy Cox and David Steele made this cheering discovery in the summer of 1983 when, as grass-roots rockers with The Beat, they watched their meal ticket explode with all the grace of a rotten plum. Long months of internal disharmony, and a thorough disenchantment

with the constant slog around the United States, culminated in an inevitable split. In almost every publication from *The Sun* to *Melody Maker*, "musical and personal differences" were cited as primary reasons for the band's demise.

Though accurate in the broadest sense, this popular press euphemism failed to convey exactly how far and how fast The Beat's closed community had deteriorated. As the musicians suffered, so had their music. Short years before, The Beat had entered a grim new decade riding high on the crest of a dance-crazy ska revival. Yet of all the bands to appear during that brief era, they were the ones least likely to become exhausted by the frenetic Two-Tone bop. They were tipped to succeed. Great things were expected of them. The sublime 'Drowning', one of The Beat's later singles, showed that they were more than capable of pushing far ahead of the rocksteady Prince Buster crowd, only by this time the band had already fallen prey to a debilitating album-tour-album cycle. It left them too stressed, too drained, and with far too little time to write even passably good songs. In short, the process precluded any musical creativity whatsoever.

Nevertheless, the group were still expected to pluck fresh melodies out of thin air, write disarming lyrics, listen to the resulting slurry with a critical ear, and piece together definitive versions in the studio without the songs having had so much as half a chance to mature. Those balmy days of allowing 'Best Friend', 'Twist And Crawl' and 'Mirror In The Bathroom' to ferment in Birmingham's Mercat Cross pub were long past. Time and space away from each other, and the demands of an omnipresent record company, would have alleviated tensions to some extent, but the chemistry had already begun to sour . . . "We spent most of the time being complete bastards to one another."

Then the drug-induced indolence set in. To their horror the band awoke to find themselves performing drunk or worse on stage, simply in order to get through another set of embarrassing, half-baked tunes. "Which was a shame, really," David told *No.1*'s Karen Swayne, "because the first year with The Beat was fun. We were all very young, just left school and started a group, and the next thing we knew we were on *Top Of The Pops*. But it went on too long. Looking back on it we should have split up three years before we actually did. Now the bad memories have taken over from the good ones."

The irony was that The Beat's creative nadir, not to mention their complete lack of self-esteem, coincided with their commercial zenith. This was especially true in America, where the real money was. 'Special Beat Service', the group's third and final LP, astonished everybody – bar their American record company – by notching up sales of nearly half a million. In global terms it went on to become their biggest-selling LP. To this day, members of the long-dissolved partnership are still given annual accounts to sign. Not surprisingly, hard-nosed Miles Copeland, boss of their American label IRS, was gutted by this bombshell. He told the band in no uncertain terms that they were mad to split up now, reminding them that the smallest audience they had played to was 8,000. Their return trip would see crowds of 50,000 turning out to see The English Beat! Why, they'd all be millionaires by the end of next year . . .!

But Copeland's pleas for unity fell on deaf ears. The group had had enough. The party was over and they all had a long walk home. Rumours of an impending break-up had been common currency since the appearance of their mediocre 'Special Beat Service' album back in October 1982. Even to the untrained ear it was obvious that The Beat were well past their sell-by date. For the pundits, however, there were a few anxious moments. A re-working of Andy Williams' 'Can't Get Used To Losing You' coasted to number three in the UK singles charts during May 1983, and following a stint as support on The Police's US tour, David Bowie employed The Beat to warm up the multitude at his open air concert in Milton Keynes. Such exposure hardly signalled the beginning of the end.

Then one July morning a letter arrived, a 'dear John' letter. Circularised by the band's lawyers, it informed the remaining Beat members that Dave Wakeling and Ranking Roger, the group's irrepressible vocal duo, had resigned. It also transpired that the pair had already set up shop as General Public, having had both the good fortune and good foresight to secure a recording deal with Virgin Records before tendering their resignations. A *fait accompli* indeed. And one in which the clandestine manoeuvring had not gone down terribly well with the others – "Let's just say they don't come round for tea any more."

More than simply out of character, this guilt-ridden secrecy made a mockery of the group's much-vaunted cards-on-the-table democracy. It rankled for a while, but though they found themselves unexpectedly without gainful employ, David Steele and Andy Cox's overriding feelings were of utter relief. The last three months, they declared, had been absolute hell. "When I realised it was over I thought – great!" David revealed to *Melody Maker*'s Ian Pye. "Everything had become impossible. It was awful. It was like having a terrible relationship with a girlfriend – once it's over it's like a deliverance."

As it happened, July 1983 turned out to be a good month for bands to part company. Terry Hall, the sunken-eyed ex-Special, disbanded his second outfit, Fun Boy Three, and Paul Weller orphaned parka wearers the length and breadth of the country when he kicked The Jam into touch in order to pursue a more mellow arrangement with The Style Council. General Public, too, set out on a similar, flexible path. Enlisting the help of The Clash's Mick Jones, Aswad's brass section, The Specials' Horace Gentleman, and a couple of Dexy's, the group were up and running before Christmas. Their self-titled début single appeared in March 1984. Predictably, General Public's Dave Wakeling and Ranking Roger, donning dapper blue boilersuits, soaked up all the press attention formerly bestowed on The Beat. Their 'All The Rage' LP was well received in America, but these prime movers failed to shift adequate numbers of either feet

THE SWEET & THE SOUR

or units at home, impressing neither critics nor the public at large. Before 1984 was over the breakaway faction had disappeared out of earshot.

Meanwhile, their former colleagues, bassist David Steele and guitarist Andy Cox, whom the music papers had all but given up for lost, were happily ensconced in their respective Handsworth homes. For the time being they were content to pursue quiet, normal lives, something they hadn't been able to do in a long time.

"We go out, see old friends," said David. "And we've even got a normal barber again." Though life for the two of them had become one long round of tea drinking and cinema-going, interrupted by occasional visits to one of the local curry houses or an expedition to Birmingham's Rag Market in search of new clothes, the urge to make music remained strong. Shortly after The Beat split, Andy and David hit upon the idea for a new band. Its sound, they fancied, would weave the scrawny articulacy of jazz with a weft of classic soul power. To remain shackled to the whine and grind of yesterday's style was simply out of the question. The problem was that the desired effect would be impossible to achieve without a good strong vocalist, and since neither of them would let the other within 50 yards of a microphone, they would have to start recruiting. Not that either of these modestly accomplished musicians looked upon this as being any great obstacle. After all, singers were 10 a penny, weren't they . . .? Little did they know that their search for a dynamic vocalist to front their mute and nameless outfit would keep both of them occupied well into the New Year.

Andy Cox and David Steele first met on the Isle of Wight, David's birthplace, back in the summer of 1978. One of the island's few teenage castaways with fashionably short hair, up-to-the-minute music tastes and a rudimentary understanding of the bass guitar, David was inspired to answer an invitation in the local rag to "shake some action." Half expecting to be met at the appointed time by some local no-hoper, he was pleasantly surprised to be greeted by Andy Cox and Dave Wakeling, a pair of solar panel builders and would-be musicians *en vacance* from darkest Birmingham. Back at his hosts' holiday lodgings, David introduced himself more informally by bad-mouthing their record collection. The rest, as they say, is history.

Eagerly, the southerner shipped out and The Beat were born. After-hours practices in, among other places, the basement of Winson Green's All Saints Hospital where David was training as a psychiatric nurse, eventually paid off. Gigs soon followed and when BBC Radio's most influential disc jockey, John Peel, was moved to trade cheques with the band – as the top name on the

DESPERATELY SEEKING ROLAND

bill he alone earned four times more than the lean and hungry Beat troupe – they sensed that success was just around the corner. Next stop, the offices of Two-Tone Records and the release of 'Tears Of A Clown' . . . Now, some five years on from that first encounter, it was David's turn to be the waiting partner on a blind date. The obvious avenues were explored, but unfortunately adverts placed in the 'Musicians Wanted' columns of the British music press produced quantity rather than quality. Recalling the process to *Melody Maker*'s Ian Pye, David said that initially both he and Andy were quite blasé about the task of finding a new singer.

"We thought we'd just put an ad in the papers, and all these young Al Greens and James Browns would arrive. But it was just bozo after bozo!" Complacency evaporated and obsession set in, and as time went by their quest assumed epic proportions. David vaguely imagined their model vocalist to be "the new Otis Redding," yet if they were unable to find an even remotely suitable candidate close to home, he and Andy would have to look to the United States, home of their favourite singers. Across the great divide, however, the story proved much the same. It soon became apparent that throughout the entire American continent there were no budding Marvin Gayes, a dearth of aspiring Sam Cookes and even fewer nascent Elvis Presleys. The only benefit of an advertisement run on their behalf by MTV, the colony's all-day video jukebox, was that it kept the postman busy in Birmingham's postal district 21. Literally hundreds of cassettes dropped onto the mat, an unhealthy diet of young Bob Segers and Bruce Springsteens which soon had our heroes reaching for the Rennies.

"I used to listen to them every morning before breakfast," moaned David. "And they would put me in a bad mood for the rest of the day . . . There weren't even any worthwhile female vocalists. I suppose one of them might have been the new Aretha Franklin, but if she was, we didn't recognise her."

Still, the exercise kept Andy and David in blank tapes for years, and they had a good laugh at some of the photographs which they'd insisted the applicants send in. After all, the pop industry was nothing if not image conscious, and if they were to succeed again, their singer would have to have good looks as well as vocal talent. David confessed to *NME*'s Adrian Thrills that in a more desperate moment the pair had even tried their hand at poaching. Flying to the States, he met up with Bernie Fowler, itinerant vocalist from the early eighties electro era who appeared on singles by Shango, Rock It Band and, most notably, The Peech Boys' 'Don't Make Me Wait'. "It was

THE SWEET & THE SOUR

never a practical idea," conceded David. "But we approached him because we were grasping at straws by that point. We'd heard that he was angling to leave The Peech Boys and we thought we'd try and pinch him. We'd heard some of his stuff and knew he had a really strong voice, but it simply wasn't practical having a singer based in New York."

Back in Handsworth, despondency was beginning to set in. One evening Andy and David were slumped in front of the television when a figure appeared on screen who reminded them of one Roland Gift, erstwhile saxophonist-cum-singer with The Ackrylix, a non-league ska outfit from Hull who had supported The Beat in days of yore. Oddly, as *No.1*'s Deanne Pearson learned, Mr Gift's dancing had made a more lasting impression on the pair than his voice.

"We remembered Roland mainly because of the way he moved," regaled Andy. "And how he looked. But it turned out he could sing really well . . . Then we found out he wrote lyrics, too." Being shy, retiring chaps, David and Andy had to persuade Andy's wife to *make that call!* Somewhat bemused, yet eager to further his singing career, Roland agreed to an audition. Though he hadn't even begun to realise his potential with The Ackrylix, Roland had always considered himself to be the best of the band's three singers. As it turned out, the 'audition' was more of an informal meeting, complete with tea and biscuits, during which the respective parties quickly warmed to one another. Roland's prospective employers enlarged upon their ideas for the new band and at the end of the meeting Roland was entrusted with a tape containing a few backing tracks. His brief was simple: listen to the tape and come up with some lyrics by next week. The following week he sang.

Of those original songs only an embryonic version of 'Move To Work' survived the months of spit and polish which followed. Roland was in, they needed no further convincing. In David's opinion, they had unearthed . . . "the best male singer in England."

"I thought he was a charming young man," he told *NME*'s Alan Jackson. "Once we found Roland, the doors were locked."

Up until this time, 21-year-old Roland Gift had been living in less than salubrious surroundings in the Holloway area of London, where a rent strike in protest against latter-day Rachmanism inspired bricks to come raining down the chimney, courtesy of an understanding landlord. It was all part of life's rich tapestry for the Humberside ex-punk, who had moved to the Capital in search of his proverbial fortune. Roland had breezed through a few years before as a teenage rock and roll gypsy in pursuit of his idols The Clash. A familiar yet striking face in the crowd – dark skinned, with hair dyed red, yellow and green: rasta coloured – he had been enlisted to assemble the stage backdrop at The Clash's prestigious Music Machine gigs in Camden Town.

Back in Hull, Roland's home town, fashions changed rapidly from punk to mod, and Roland, with his hair newly two-toned down, skanked along to 1979's unprecedented ska explosion. His head of bleached blond hair soon earned him the nickname Guinness, and the boundless energy of ska's second coming lured him out of the audience and on to the stage amid The Ackrylix. Though the group made no lasting impression on the sta-prest generation's collective imagination, they did manage to commit one stage favourite, 'Dangerman', to vinyl. Once The Ackrylix had gone the way of all flesh, Roland channelled his creative energies into acting. Drama having been what he referred to as his "saving grace" at school, Roland developed his talents still further, working with the Hull Community Theatre Workshop, performing mainly in improvised plays which the company took around to schools and other local venues.

"We did one play in a mental hospital," he told *No.1*'s Paul Simper. "That was really bizarre. We did a thirties cabaret thing for them. Some of the inmates got into it though. I sang the Al Jolson song 'Mammy', and the supervisor of the place said he saw this really introverted girl singing along. That was a nice touch." But it wasn't long before Roland took his destiny in his hands, recklessly turning his back on a promising career as a worker in a fish factory, and headed south young man down the A1. In London, however, he found himself torn between two passions.

"When I moved to London," he recalled to *Melody Maker*'s Dean Haynes, "I had to make a decision, and I chose music because it's a lot more immediate. You can start tomorrow, whereas to do acting, it's a lot more institutionalised – you know, you're expected to go to drama school. Music is a lot more open and free." Roland earned his keep at a day job working a stall in Camden market selling racy lacy underwear. If legend was not in the habit of telling porkies, he also bared all as a male stripper at hen parties for £50 a time. However, Roland's evenings and weekends were usually, if less profitably, spent in a more creative vein fronting a Rhythm 'n' Pub band, The Bones. It was the kind of band that could be heard week in week out clear across the Great Wen from Cockfosters to Croydon, bands without whom the harmonica would have soon become extinct.

For Roland, the invitation from rock 'n' pop veterans Steele and Cox couldn't have come at a better time. "When they told me what they were after it sounded really good," learned *Record Mirror*'s Andy Strike. "I was playing in this blues band around the London circuit and I didn't like it at all, so this was a great opportunity to get away from that for a start. Then when I

THE SWEET & THE SOUR

FYC **16**

started working with them, they were the best people I'd ever worked with."

Only one problem remained and that was a matter of logistics. Roland lived in London and the group's founding fathers lived a hundred miles distant in the Midlands, hardly an ideal arrangement for a band to begin working together, let alone get to know one another. So Roland, in order to fulfil his duties as vocalist and wordsmith, committed himself to commuting to Birmingham on a weekly basis, travelling back and forth to the city which had been his childhood home.

Like David, who was the eldest of four, and Andy, who had two sisters, Roland too came from a large family. One of five children, his mother was white and his father came from the Caribbean island of St. Kitts – not an easy union in Britain during the sixties.

DESPERATELY SEEKING ROLAND

Roland remembered how they used to get spat at in the streets of Birmingham. At the age of 11, Roland, together with his brothers and sisters, transferred to Hull, where they were subsequently abandoned by their father. Though the subject of his father's leaving was understandably not open to discussion, Roland did tell *Rolling Stone* reporter Steve Pond that it was his mother who provided for the children, largely through dealing in bric-a-brac and curios. "I was always embarrassed to bring anybody home," he recalled, "because our house was just full of junk. You could hardly see the carpet."

In Birmingham, Andy would welcome him one week while David would offer him a choice of floor or sofa the next. Roland likened it to joining the Army, being thrown in together. And as the Fine Young Cannibals they got on famously. "He's a good man, I can tell you," Andy told *Smash Hits* writer William Shaw. "He does the washing up." "He doesn't do the washing up at my place," complained David. "Well, nobody does the washing up at your place!" countered Roland.

Socially, as well as artistically, Roland acted as a catalyst within the group. His mania for health and fitness had no less an influence on his new companions' lives than his lyrical contributions had on their music. Whilst he drew the line at jogging or pumping iron, preferring the spiritual step-back-and-repulse-the-monkey of tai chi, Roland was determined to pull his musicians into shape with regular swimming sessions at the local baths. Unable to bear Roland's sniffy, "Can't you do better than that?" as they completed a feeble five lengths, Andy and David soon improved to a respectable half mile or more. There were dietary considerations also. Typically sceptical to begin with, David soon found himself eating muesli for breakfast like the best of them. "Well, I just don't want to turn into one of those ugly old slobs. You see a lot of groups that are really disgusting. Some of these people look 40 when they're only 30."

The band's all-important name was

THE SWEET & THE SOUR

Andy's doing. Tossing aside a well-thumbed Thesaurus, Andy picked up an obscure tome entitled *Jazz In The Movies*. It told of a box office flop made in 1960 starring Pearl Bailey, and Robert Wagner as a trumpet player. Called *All The Fine Young Cannibals*, *Halliwell's Film Guide* damned the picture in biblical tones: "The glum joys of sex and dope in the big city are revealed in this boring rather than daring farrago which is not even unintentionally funny."

Andy's suggestion, unlike the movie, was greeted with unanimous approval. They also chose the name, said Andy, because . . . "it was so weird that nobody would sue us over it." Wrong. Apparently there was another bunch of man-eaters on the loose, named simply The Cannibals, a garage-band of unremarkable ordinariness. All the same, Fine Young Cannibals found themselves taken to court as their first single ascended the charts. Needless to say, Fine Young Cannibals won the day, not that the original Cannibals were satisfied at being laughed out of court. A cheeky single later appeared by a group calling themselves the Five Young Cannibals. Obviously they were bad losers. With the initial help of ex-Beat drummer Everett Morton, the core of three Fine Young Cannibals was now off the mark.

Presently, however, Everett the family man took early retirement, making way for Martin Parry whose high calibre drumming was well known to Andy through his involvement with another band on the local Birmingham scene. Similarly, Saxa, The Beat's old faithful mascot saxophonist, who also contributed during the Fine Young Cannibals' early days, eventually found himself having to make way for a younger man as a long illness, exacerbated by an intemperate love of brandy, forced him to bow out. Saxa's replacement, trumpet player Graeme Hamilton, came highly recommended by the saxman himself. He was the son of one of his close circle of musician friends, whose credits, like those of Saxa, read like a who's who of black music. Graeme Hamilton's superb playing was the antithesis of that lethargic, pot-bellied, white session musician school which the Fine Young Cannibals looked upon with absolute dread.

With Graeme and Martin in the fold they would never settle for second best in anything. Working at an unhurried pace, a modest collection of bittersweet songs gradually took shape. Powerful melodies buoyed Roland's plaintive vocals, the ideal foil for horn and keyboard embellishments which were kept to a strict and refreshing minimum. By the same token, Andy kept his guitar playing pure and simple. Why make music more complicated? In one of barely a handful of interviews given by Fine Young Cannibals prior to hitting the big time, Andy disclosed a fragment of the new band's musical ethos to *NME*'s Adrian Thrills.

"There was a definite decision to use proper instruments rather than some great wodge of synthesised gunge," he said. "And I've always hated that raunchy rock guitar sound. Even in The Beat we never really went close to that. If anything, that's the thing that's changed least since The Beat. We've never really been into axing out! But I wouldn't say we're the only group that have ever felt like that. If you listen to early Talking Heads singles, there's a very similar feel to the guitar sound."

Working from a mutually understood reference point, their music was in the first instance unashamedly soul-inspired. It was, however, widely informed, with a wealth of diverse, and occasionally perverse, influences soon coming into play. From Hindi film soundtracks to The Shangri-La's and Jacques Brell to Andy's yen for Arabic music, Fine Young Cannibals were able to draw on a comprehensive musical vocabulary. "But when people ask me what we play I usually say soul music," commented Roland. "That's closest to what it is, but it doesn't really sum up what the band are like."

David was quick to point out Fine Young Cannibals were definitely not part of the current trend for nostalgia. Assimilating a collection of rare-but-groovy soul records was certainly rewarding, but that alone would scarcely disturb the cobwebs. Neither were new 'jazz' bands like Everything But The Girl, Carmel and Weekend the spearhead of a defiant new direction in music. They sounded on occasion as though they'd just happened upon their parents' old Charlie Parker and Stan Getz albums whilst practising in the attic. Sade was getting closer, but her cool, varnished melodies lacked that vital punch. "The thing I don't like about those groups," complained David, "is that they seem really wary of putting any effort into anything. They all seem frightened to break into a sweat. They do everything too carefully, rather than just relying on feel."

Whilst the two musicians were on fairly familiar territory as they composed the tunes, Roland was delighted to find himself breaking new ground both as a vocalist and more especially as a lyricist. For the first time in his experience, Roland was able to set his own words to a musical style which complemented his voice perfectly and gave him the freedom to really sing. "A lot of the groups I've been in during the past were far more rockish," affirmed Roland. "Which isn't good for a singer. You just can't hear yourself in that kind of band. I've always wanted to sing, what I needed was a band that would enable me to do that in the way I wanted to."

His lyrics, rooted firmly in that unpretentious middle ground between the intellectual and the naïve, echoed the music's strength and simplicity. 'Move To Work' was a prime example of this. Its subject was that of a young couple whose only way forward was for the man to cross the north/south divide in search of a job. The cheerless prospect of sustaining their love through remittance payments, a common practice for many families, was handled in such a way that any kernel of a 'message' or 'meaning' was swathed appealingly in easy phrases. But this never dulled the bite . . . 'I wish there was another way for us, for you and me my love; but if I miss this train, there won't be another; and if I get there late, they'll say don't you bother.'

Such well-observed couplets conveyed a sense and sincerity that far outclassed any three-minute treatise on humanity or the perpetual emotion of casual sex-beat singles. Roland's strongest imagery was invariably generated when writing about physical or emotional displacement, his most recurrent themes. *Sounds*' Dave Henderson was later moved to comment . . . "They may joke between themselves about going out and living it, then sitting down and putting their experiences into their music, but it's that very personal edge which sets Fine Young Cannibals apart from the many young pretenders."

Fine Young Cannibals knew they had the right stuff. Now all they had to do was convince a commercial music world awed by the rogue elephants of rock, U2, and dominated by charismatic figures like Michael Jackson, Madonna, Boy George, George Michael *et al*. Not forgetting those new kids on the block, Frankie Goes To Hollywood. Certainly there was an impressive number of Goths gathering in the wings – slow, crow-black types who, in adopting rock's fetish for leather, appeared to be nothing more than bikers without bikes – but the British record industry kept their hands firmly in their pockets. They flirted briefly with sham psychedelia, youths sporting long fringes and paisley waistcoats playing spangly guitars, but this was way before The Stone Roses were so much as darling buds in the garden.

Eventually big business cottoned on to the sound of urban America, which wasn't just glitzy disco music dressed up in fashionably torn jeans, sneakers and

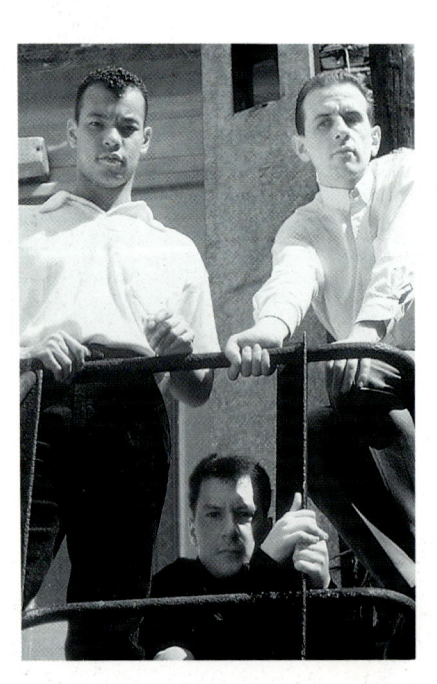

THE SWEET & THE SOUR

baseball hats. No sir. This was the authentic sound of the eighties. Electro, break-dance, rap, hip-hop, house, swingbeat were all strains of a new kind of street music that evolved and mutated so rapidly that these labels fell into disuse faster than they had achieved hipness.

Such was the state of play when, in July 1984, Andy, Roland and David decided to break cover. The band were featured on the front of *Black Music* magazine and *Sounds* ran a suitably purposeful photo of the trio, unsmiling and soberly dressed, plus the footnote 'Out To Lunch'. The accompanying paragraph informed the readership that Fine Young Cannibals were on the prowl: "So far they are still talking with record companies but there are no records scheduled as yet. They plan to start recording as soon as they've finalised a deal." Finalised indeed.

At that point in time, Fine Young Cannibals were without a manager and totally fed up with casting their pearls before swine as they hawked a demo round every worthwhile record company in the land. Recorded at Birmingham's Outlaw Studios, their tape contained three songs: 'Move To Work', 'Like A Stranger' and 'Couldn't Care More'. Later a fourth, 'Johnny Come Home', was added but still they continued to be turned down.

Zang Tum Tum, home of techno-funsters Art Of Noise and assorted derivatives, not to mention the once-enormous and ever so naughty Frankie Goes To Hollywood, were one of the few companies to lend them an ear. ZTT overlord Paul 'Slyboots' Morley listened to both their demo and title music recently composed by Andy and David for Channel Four's political documentary, *State Of The World*. The soundtrack featured a cut-up rap taken from speeches made by Ronald Reagan, which eventually surfaced as an FYC B-side, 'Good Times And Bad'. Anyway, Channel Four rejected it on the grounds that it was too biased and ZTT turned the band down for other, undisclosed, sorry fellas reasons. A few months later, Frankie Goes To Hollywood had their second number one smash with 'Two Tribes', a song whose vocal was reportedly based on, yes, you've guessed it, speeches by the US President. At the time, Andy, Roland and David thought it was nothing more than coincidence. Now, looking back, this coincidence was a touch too close to the edit for comfort. Sour grapes? Relax . . .

The few paltry offers Fine Young Cannibals did receive wouldn't have kept a one-legged man in shoe polish. One label, London Records, offered the group a £5000/two singles deal, but the group were really angling for an album contract. They knew that if they could release an album, their material would stand up and sing for itself. But the record company wouldn't come across. Unfortunately, what little reputation they ought to have been able to trade off – "Hi! Two of us used to be in this band, y'know, and we had, like, five Top 10 singles and two number three albums!" – was nullified by General Public having proved about as popular as a side order of garlic bread at the Vampires' Annual Dinner And Dance. As a consequence, wary music business mandarins shunned this second reincarnation from last year's flavour of the month – in some cases three times – as a potential bad debt.

This matter of their public rebirth was beginning to cause David no little embarrassment. "I hate the idea of being a spin-off band," he groused. "Bands that form from old chart bands are usually a load of crap." For the time being they would just have to suffer their own enthusiasm for themselves eclipsing that of any prospective patron. Having thus failed in their first attempt to get back onto the magic roundabout, David and Andy began to feel sorry for Roland, the innocent party, as it were. Still, if the worst came to the worst, he could always work in a shoe shop and they could go on the dole.

A common prejudice the group came up against was that the Artistes and Repertoire people couldn't hear enough state-of-the-art technology. They were all too quick to damn the singer, the songs and the musicians. Frankly, Fine Young Cannibals were too acoustic, too unsophisticated, too orthodox for prevalent market tastes.

"It was weird," recalled Andy. "Everybody said, 'Oh, soul isn't that trendy. Can you stick a few more drum machines and synthesisers on it?" David immediately went on the defensive about the 'old soul' tag. Then again, such a label might have been construed as a back-handed compliment: most 'modern' soul was sentimental slush by comparison. "Our music isn't revivalist," he told *The Hit*'s Richard Lowe. "I think it's true that we may give the impression of sounding old-fashioned, but if you play our songs next to an old Four Tops record or something, there's definitely a big difference. I think it's the voice more than anything that people link with that era."

The rejections smarted, but the trio were unwilling to make these or any other creative compromises. To impose gridiron rhythms on their fluid arrangements, pepper them with impertinent burps from a digital sequencer and then douse it all with gratuitous synthesiser washes would have brought Fine Young Cannibals unto the world as yet more vendors of homogenised pop. Wisely, they listened to their own advice: try the back door, it's usually unlocked. So, with a video camera and a couple of pink guitars for props, Fine Young Cannibals set about engineering their big break.

Recorded in Birmingham, their shoestring video was premièred in March 1985 on what was then the small screen's foremost pop magazine, *The Tube*. The results were startling. A brief and characteristically garbled introduction from presenter Jools Holland announced the Fine Young Cannibals,

THE SWEET & THE SOUR

whoever they were, and the band promptly burst into song with 'Johnny Come Home'. What the viewers saw was a young Lee Van Cleef, complete with widow's peak but minus the moustache, accompanied by a fine pair of Cyrano de Bergerac noses, lots of wobbly legs, and foreheads to match Phil Collins'. What they heard was sweet sweet music. On came the adverts and the Channel Four switchboard was jammed with calls from people all asking the same question: "Where can we buy this record?"

As *Jamming*'s Bruce Dessau subsequently noted, the dormant hive began to buzz: "It's a funny old world where a record company's idea of scouting for new talent is to turn on Channel Four on a Friday night." But that was precisely how Fine Young Cannibals got themselves 'discovered'. Or more precisely, rediscovered. Eyes shed their scales and suddenly the group were inundated with wonderful offers from those self-same record companies who had ushered them so unceremoniously out of the door just a few months previously.

"TV kind of canonises you," said David, cynically. "It makes you into some kind of musical saint. And of course, most things are so bad, anything half-decent seems like the second coming." To say that their television début caused something of a stir would be a gross understatement. Listening to the Cannibals' demo anew, record companies such as CBS were moved to wave what were in essence blank cheques in front of them. When pressed as to the actual figures involved the group's reply was a coy chuckle. Were we talking telephone numbers here? – "Oh yes, definitely! We could have taken some deals and simply retired on the advance . . ." The deal they eventually settled for came from – ahem – London Records.

Apart from an immodest sum of money and maximum support, London was prepared to offer Fine Young Cannibals a considerable degree of artistic control over everything from their 'corporate image', videos and album covers, right down to the lowly tour passes. To underestimate this latter freedom would be to misjudge the people involved, to believe that theirs was not the guiding hand. London also allowed the group to conduct themselves pretty much as they wished while signed to the label, particularly with regard to vinyl output and, more pertinently, methods of promotion. With the nightmare of The Beat's Stateside tours still not exorcised from their memories, Andy and David were adamant that their relaunched careers wouldn't hip-hop, skip and jump from single to album to slow-agonising-death world tour. Roland, on the other hand, tended to view the obligatory contractual donkey-work in a more pragmatic light.

"You're doing a lot of work," he told *No.1*'s Mike Hrano, "but really you're not reaching that many people. Not compared to, say, doing *Top Of The Pops* or *The Tube*. Just three minutes on the right TV programme can get to more people than watch you on tour."

Though they were primarily concerned with cutting a single, and indeed preferred to remain cloistered in the recording studio, the seminal Cannibals graciously made a few live appearances during the first half of 1985. They performed both in their home town and in the Capital, where an encouraging turnout at Soho's Wag Club even brought a few curious celebrities out of the woodwork. "Sean Connery turned up and he seemed to like what we do," remarked David. "There were a load of poxy musicians there, too . . ."

Where it normally took months to record, press, package and deliver a single to the shops, Fine Young Cannibals' peach reached the market place in a fraction of the time. They could have released what was the ripest song in their repertoire even sooner had they not succumbed to the temptation of an attractive and terribly fashionable hi-tech production. Initial attempts at recording 'Johnny Come Home' under the auspices of Ann Dudley, a slick techno-pop producer hewn from the same flawless rock as ZTT's Trevor Horn, proved to be both a creative and an ideological blind alley. David complained to *NME*'s Adrian Thrills that she seemed hell-bent on ironing out their idiosyncrasies, erasing their identities even. "We will try anything once," he sighed. "So when the record company suggested her we went along with it. It sounded like a fun idea to combine a soul base with a pop production, but in the end it was a waste of time. She wanted everything clean and exactly in time. She didn't understand feel at all . . . She even thought it was strange that Andy and I wanted to play on the record. She would rather have got all her friends in to play the parts!"

Prudently, they ditched the project and the Ann Dudley monstermix (featuring Fine Young Cannibals) never came to pass. Ann Dudley went on to have a longer working relationship with Lloyd Cole And The Commotions, and in place of what would have been a fine tune despoiled by unsympathetic paw prints, the record-buying public were treated to Fine Young Cannibals' self-produced demo. Recorded at the Sound Suite, where The Beat's first two hits were also made, their own hand-tinted version of 'Johnny Come Home' contained beautiful quirks and plenty of kick. " 'Johnny Come Home'," wrote *Jamming*'s Bruce Dessau, "is a heady blend of clickety guitars, muted trumpets and bubbling bass, with just a hint of northern soul to encourage frequent flexing of the feet."

"The idea for the song," revealed Andy, "came from a TV documentary of the same name which was shown years and years ago. It was about young people from the north coming down to London thinking that the streets are paved with gold discs and they're not."

Released in June, their single leapt clean out of the radio and straight up the charts. Its winning touch was a subtle pincer movement performed by Roland's voice and Graeme Hamilton's trumpet solitary, evincing midnight roads empty and glistening after the rain. If The Pet Shop Boys hadn't romped to victory at the year's end with 'West End Girls', 'Johnny Come Home' would have easily been the outstanding début of 1985. The band hoped it was the kind of record that would be bought by people who hadn't been near a record shop in years, having become disaffected with an atrophied alternative scene and perennial daytime radio blandness. Many commentators remarked on the single's apparent spontaneity, drawing attention to the fact that it had been recorded and mixed in under 24 hours. What they were ignoring were the months of arduous groundwork and meticulous refinement prior to their emergence from a wilderness of rehearsal rooms. *Melody Maker*'s Ian Pye noted that David's patience and Andy's determination were to a certain extent compensating for those years of relative anonymity as The Beat's obscured anchormen.

"Because we were always in the background I knew we would have to be something special to make people notice," asserted David. "That's why we've taken our time, made sure everything was how we wanted it. If we'd released an average single it would have meant death for us, I'm sure."

Fine Young Cannibals had reached base camp. *Smash Hits*' William Shaw joined David, Roland and Andy as they huddled round Andy's black and white portable television for *Top Of The Pops*' crucial chart rundown. When the presenter beamed . . . "This week's highest climber, up 19 places to Number 16! Fine Young Cannibals!" . . . the relief was almost palpable.

"This is it," they gasped, "everything we've worked up to since we left school. And if this cocks up then God knows . . . Then we're all a bunch of, um, silly damn fellows!"

MAD ABOUT THE BOYS

In marked contrast to the low-key live affairs of recent weeks, an exhaustive round of trans-European television appearances was scheduled to coincide with the release of 'Johnny Come Home'. These began at home with Fine Young Cannibals popping up on breakfast television, the children's Saturday morning show *Razzmatazz*, and as surprise special guest stars on *Wogan*, the BBC's cosy tea-time chat show. Drunk and happy, Roland and his elasticated sidekicks provided the entertainment whilst genial host Terry polished his smile and upwards of 10 million viewers digested their evening meal. "We were hoping for an audience with His Grace," joked Andy, "but unfortunately it was not to be . . . Actually, we only saw the back of his head."

By late summer 1985, 'Johnny Come Home' had spent three months in the domestic charts, reaching a high point of number eight in July. When subsequently released across the Channel, it charted in almost every European country from the Mediterranean to the Baltic. Fine Young Cannibals, in hot pursuit of their hit single, skipped across one continental border after another, dutifully performing their spindle-shanks routine through a succession of three-minute pop slots. Miming didn't bother them particularly, so long as they didn't have to do it in front of a studio audience which made them feel a bit daft. The audience didn't seem to mind either way: 'Johnny Come Home' made the Top Five in Holland, Germany, Italy and Finland, the latter coup being achieved in the wake of a Helsinki gig being broadcast live on radio throughout Scandinavia.

Evidently, the song's drive and sparkle lost nothing in translation. Their spunky little tune also made the Top 20 in Australia, the kind of bizarre aside that warmed the Cannibals' cockles. Prior to these promotional excursions, Roland confessed that he had only been abroad once before, to Amsterdam on a day trip – and that had been for the Duty Frees rather than the culture. So whereas he was able to take in the brief snatches of local colour afforded between airport and hotel, an old lag like Andy could only recall Fine Young Cannibals' first commercial adventure somewhat hazily. "Every time I hear 'Johnny Come Home'," he told *No.1*'s Karen Swayne, "I go into a weird trance and think I'm on a foreign TV show!"

In the autumn the group began to spend a greater proportion of their time back in Britain, where the relative tranquility of piecing together a début LP went undisturbed, save for a rash of interviews from various interested parties. One of the undoubted success stories of 1985, Fine Young Cannibals were now embraced quite unreservedly from all sides of the critical spectrum and gently coerced into giving a full account of themselves. Glossy melt-in-your-mouth-not-in-your-hands teen magazines questioned this latest bunch of happening guys on their likes and dislikes, clothes and quiffs; and the weighty yet increasingly chart-conscious broadsheets probed their processes creative, personal and, more especially, political. FYC trivia came thick and fast. Tennessee Ernie Ford's '16 Tons' had been at number one when Andy, the eldest member of the band, was born. David, the middle one, had come into the world to the strains of The Shadows' chart topping instrumental, 'Apache'. And Roland, the baby of the group, first exercised his lungs to the Elvis Presley hit, 'Good Luck Charm'. Such pedigree . . .

An affable threesome, Andy, Roland and David were pleasant, approachable, and decidedly more articulate than the flimsy, one-dimensional chart acts who won a few column inches of wasted publicity before being engulfed in the quicksands of pop, never to be featured again. "We're quite well respected," Roland told *The Hit*'s Ro Newton. "And we're also a chart band. I think that's an enviable position."

Only one sore point remained, aggravated by persistent reference to their omnipresent past, namely The Beat. Stoically, Andy and David would try to play down their ranking roots. They did not wish the connection to taint their renaissance in any way: "That was just an apprenticeship, where we made our mistakes. Now we've got to act like we've died and been reincarnated." Once the tale of the downward spiral had been recounted a few score times and 10, sleeping dogs were left to lie and David, for one, would begin to divulge information most readily. At that time, he came across as the most voluble member of the band, volunteering opinions on everything from Page Three girls to Jeffrey Archer to Japanese food, all with laconic good humour.

The balance of the Cannibals' facts and fancies was supplied by a thoroughly ingenuous Roland. Though he was the undisputed centre of attention on stage or on camera, Roland had not yet had a similar role thrust upon him in an interview situation. In fact, in the very beginning he was worried that people might regard him simply as Andy and David's backing singer. Heaven forbid! Of the three interviewees, Roland was the most energetic and cheerful, the man most willing to play ball. At least until the journalist either flagged or ran out of time, or the make-up girl gave them the signal for the all-important photo-session. Having their picture taken was definitely the least wearisome of the band's self-promotional duties.

"I mean," grinned Roland, "I'd be a liar if I said that being in magazines wasn't attractive!" The group appeared to tire only when the volume of interviews increased to such a point that they were treading water, answering questions they had heard a hundred times before. When this happened, they would playfully embellish the party line, saying that Roland had been discovered singing in some dodgy Finsbury Park bar or they were all living together in a converted Docklands warehouse – honest! But they always performed with a smile. Roland told *Smash Hits*' Mike Souter that he regarded having to justify himself as an occupational hazard, part of the rock-biz publicity machine. "But the best bit," he insisted, "is just knowing you can stay in bed if you want to. I mean, for instance, if I really didn't want to I could have said, 'I'm not going to come out today.' It's not as if I'd lose my job. It's not as if I'd ruin my chances of promotion, y'know?"

Andy, on the other hand, began to respond increasingly in interviews with wariness and reticence, unless he was participating in some three-cornered in-joke. Clearly less than enamoured of having his brains picked, Andy was unlikely to be drawn on a question like . . . "Who writes the lyrics?" let alone examine the whys and wherefores of a group he just happened to be in. Essentially, he had no wish to ascribe undue importance to what the whole group regarded as the natural, if sometimes tortuous, process of creating music. His companions, too, would have been happier on occasion to have left the trousers on their tunes. Having a song de-bagged in print held all the allure of being mooned on an overfull stomach.

The least outspoken Cannibal was perhaps the one most likely to pop. There was something in Andy's withering green-eyed gaze which hinted at

THE SWEET & THE SOUR

inner furies and an intolerance of the banal. It should not have been too much of a surprise to read in shocked tabloids that one Andy Cox had trashed the prize-giving ceremony at the annual European music industry junket, MIDEM, held in Cannes. 'Johnny Come Home' had been voted one of the best six European singles of 1985 and the band had been pledged to appear in person, not that anyone took the trouble of warning them that tacky trophies were going to be doled out. Thus compromised, Fine Young Cannibals duly found themselves on the podium under the lights. But rather than shuffle and cringe with embarrassment as Matt Bianco lifted the top award, Andy took the zero option, successfully landing a pot of yoghurt on the victor. Retaliation was swift. One of Mr Bianco's honchos nearly connected with Andy's wedding tackle, whereupon a brief mêlée ensued until the cavalry arrived in the form of alarmed officials. Exeunt Andy Cox in the opposite direction to everyone else. As luck would have it, this riotous assembly was beamed live via satellite into hundreds of thousands of homes across Europe. As a consequence, the group left the Côte d'Azur not with a nice, shiny award, but a life ban bestowed on them by MIDEM. Not that this worried them unduly. More damaging, perhaps, was the year-long ban imposed by the event's German TV sponsors, which excluded the band from appearing on any of the company's networked shows.

For some time afterwards the media grapevine carried a warning that here was a band with an attitude problem. Programme producers, who were more used to acts being open-mouthed at the prospect of just appearing on TV, suddenly became wary of the Unpredictable Young Cannibals, the most unlikely 'wild men of rock'. If the truth be known, it was more in character for the band to have a go at the opposition – or Thatcher's Britain or Rupert Murdoch – than be continually self-effacing. Fine Young Cannibals were not the Golden Boys Of Pop and did not wish to be regarded as such. The idea of becoming over-involved in the cliquey free drinks music scene was anathema to them, a bit like committing incest on a grand scale.

"We never speak to other bands," commented David. "They're all objectionable, including us . . . But we're definitely the only decent group in England today. The others are all crap: their songs, their singers, the way they play, the way they look . . ."

With certain exceptions, the group made it perfectly clear that they didn't want anyone outside the group coming much closer than shouting distance. For the sake of sanity, *Record Mirror*'s Steve Masters was told, this *cordon sanitaire* was also intended for fans, well, hangers-on. "The other night I went out for a drink with a friend," recalled Roland, "and this guy came up and said, 'I like your music.' He asked us where we were off to and when we told him he said, 'I'll come with you.' I can do without that kind of thing. I don't mind people speaking to me in the street so much, but for anyone to invite themselves to dinner . . ."

In print, bouts of surliness continued to occur from time to time, though the group's public image never really suffered for it. Andy, Roland and David were all set to become the music industry's most popular outsiders. Apart from their unmistakable, high-profile image as ascendant pop stars with natty dress sense, another picture of the Fine Young Cannibals was gradually emerging. Behind the band's occasionally superficial exterior – Andy joking about spots, David's little Lenin lapel badge, Roland's bravado about the amount of condoms he got through in a week – they were shown to be concerned but wholly unaffected individuals, embarrassed at having their commonsense views being looked upon as some kind of group manifesto. The last thing they wanted to be thought of was Angry Young Men, or worse still, Dour Young Men. They would rather volunteer to do the Eurovision Song Contest than release a string of records which were, in David's words . . . "about the Common Market or the Channel Tunnel. Or bulletins of how England's doing."

Feeling and mood were what the group excelled at, not burnt-out rhetoric. Then again, if author Sue Townsend could say with all sincerity that her book, *The Growing Pains Of Adrian Mole*, was a commentary on Britain in the eighties, then surely the trio had to accept that their known affinities and persuasions would colour almost every article on the band for some time to come. They would just have to be patient while commentators attuned themselves to their capricious, uncontrived and sometimes contradictory way of going about things. For example, rather than offer strict moral lectures – "We get more enjoyment from listening to Ken Livingstone than we do Billy Bragg!" – or strike gratuitously intimidating poses à la Public Enemy, the group favoured understatement, even the odd touch of mystery.

Early photographs bore this out. Poses were mostly on the funny side of peculiar, backs against appealingly decrepit walls, or with eyes trained on some distant celestial body. At this early stage in the game, each group member was given equal prominence. Fine Young Cannibals offered no immediate focus. Later, as Roland assumed a more dominant persona, his face would appear in intimidating close-up, with the attendant figures of Andy and David relegated to background blurs.

Their entertainment, like their image, was persuasive, unfanatical, never straying into the soggy middle-ground nor pursuing some radical extreme. Almost anyone could produce a decent rhythm just by thumping a tub. As for a tub-thumper's lyrics, they were bound to be lousy. "I don't think pop can really agitate on a political level," they told Adrian Thrills of *NME*. "If you're young and into politics, it makes more sense to join a political party than it does going to a pop concert. But I still think you can put political ideas in a pop song."

"My advice," concluded David, "is read Trotsky and listen to Burt Bacharach. It's no good listening to The Clash, you won't get any good tunes from them!"

If Fine Young Cannibals were running a Hearts and Minds campaign, they were ever mindful not to neglect the Feet. Yet it took no more than a word or an inflection to prick one's conscience: there was no denying that their music had sensitive undertones. If they actually took the plunge and sang specifically about homelessness or an uncaring government, the band were always wise to greater injustices. They wondered aloud what their happy-go-lucky peers felt when they saw programmes about striking miners or read reports about Latin American death squads. Unless they were completely cynical or fatalistic, it seemed impossible *not* to be affected by these happenings in some way. Admittedly, a bunch of lads such as themselves could at best hum a few bars of solidarity with the world's oppressed, but exactly how easy was it to ignore it all and write songs totally uncoloured by what went on around them? Or looking at it another way, was a popular musician with convictions necessarily a prat?

Thankfully, their sensibilities remained far more a part of themselves as individuals than part of their music. At a different point in time they might have been more outspoken, but not now. Twenty years ago, Vietnam would not have escaped veiled comment; 50 years ago the band might well have upped and joined the International Brigade. They were above making flabby gestures. The subject of sexism was left to those best qualified to sing about it. What the group demanded of themselves was a certain level of commitment above and against the current trend of moral lassitude. Apart from the notable exceptions of Band Aid, and its immediate successor, Live Aid, causes were generally regarded as boring and unfashionable. With an awareness of AIDS still in its infancy, a kind of charity fatigue seemed to have set in.

Without making an issue of it, Fine Young Cannibals added their voice to a 350,000 strong crowd in Paris' Place de la Concorde, where they performed at a benefit gig organised by Rock Against Racism's French counterpart. If there was any subject that the band were more likely to hold forth on, one would have expected it to be the dangerously respectable bigotry espoused by the likes of Monsieur Le Pen et cronies. In Andy, David and Roland's eyes there was nothing more invidious than racism. Roland had grown up with it and long before it had become one of The Beat's central themes, Andy and David had made their minds up about

THE SWEET & THE SOUR

cheap comments in the classroom, and later in the workplace, and the worrying growth of racist organisations which turned many youngsters' shaven heads towards the end of the seventies.

A fully paid-up member of the Labour Party Young Socialists in his youth, David attended Anti-Nazi League/Rock Against Racism 'carnivals' to demonstrate against the rise of the National Front. And to hear the bands play. He was only one among many, but this was still a fairly conscious act for a teenager from a white, middle-class backwater. Alas, the only black faces seen regularly by (impressionable) school children on the Isle of Wight were those of 'trusty' inmates from Her Majesty's Prison Parkhurst as escorted work-parties hoed and mowed the gardens of prison warders.

Contrary to what parents and parliamentarians might think, the country's youth were not naturally broad-minded let alone disciples of Nelson Mandela.

For Andy, who had been brought up in the Winson Green area of Birmingham, the question of racial integration didn't really arise. People were just people. The only type of discrimination he went in for was positive. Andy left school at 16 and went from what he described as . . . "One appalling industrial job to another." As Malu Halasa recounted in her book on The Beat, when he turned up for yet another interview, this time at a local curtain ring factory, the Barbadian boss asked him as a matter of course whether he was racially prejudiced. Andy's reply was, "Only against white people." He got the job. In all fairness, certain members of the group didn't care much for the French, but that'd be telling . . .

"Britain is a very racist country," declared David. "Much more than people think. I was trying to defend it against American friends who were saying it's racist, but then I thought, 'Why should I?'" While racism was manifestly worse in the United States than in Britain, far more openings and opportunities existed for the American black population. Which was something of a paradox in a country where the stereotypical gung-ho Moral Majority as-seen-on-TV American disliked Reds, Hispanics, Apaches, pro-abortionists, homosexuals, Iranians, Catholics and Colonel Gaddafi.

Take the thriving black music scene in the States, for example. Though it operated *apart* from the adult-orientated white rock circuit (editorial policy was such that black acts – Michael Jackson aside – rarely featured on MTV) black musicians enjoyed greater recognition and respect than, say, the UK's indigenous reggae artists. Over the years, since early sixties soul gave black culture its strongest identity outside gospel and delta blues, black music had become synonymous with racial pride. A term like ghettoblaster could only have originated in modern America. Though generally less overt in Britain, racism was in many ways more insidious. It made the nation two-faced. The inhabitants of Hong Kong were Commonwealth citizens, but entry to the mother country would be denied (by Mother Goose) because the people of Hong Kong weren't actually entitled to a British passport. So, when the Chinese took control in 1997, the Foreign Office would unplug its PC's and fax machines, cash in its Treasury Bonds and it would be thanks for the business, goodnight Kowloon. So much, then, for great British tolerance. Quite ironic really, considering the inhabitants of the British Isles were more genetically mongrelised (as the USA will become several centuries hence) than any of the ethnic minorities who found themselves on the receiving end of the natives' spurious notions of racial superiority. Jerusalem! That supposed 'blue blood' was variously Celtic, Latin, Anglo-Saxon, Danish, Norman, Jewish, Afro-Caribbean, Chinese, Asian . . .

"The Government of this country shouldn't flatter itself," sneered David. "Don't they realise that the people of Hong Kong would only consider coming to this part of the world if all else fails. I think we should let them all in. There'd be a lot more nice people around then."

So how did we acquire this endearing aspect of our national character, our xenophobia? From the days of Empire no doubt, when the East India Company acted like some voracious multi-national PLC, complete with Government backing and royal approval. The legacy of trading links established during those highly profitable colonial years has left successive 20th Century generations with a fundamental responsibility. To the Yemenis in South Shields, the Chinese in Manchester, West Indians in Cardiff's Tiger Bay, Muslims in Leicester and the scouse ancestors of a long-foundered slave trade, the most simple of human courtesies was owed. Schools in these areas have been multi-racial for upwards of 50 years, but the adults can't handle integration as well as their children can.

"There's this wonderful story which illustrates our national mentality perfectly," chuckled Andy. "Apparently, the customs hall in Amsterdam Airport used to suffer from terrible problems of congestion. At passport control there were two signs, one marked 'Dutch Nationals' and another marked 'Foreigners'. Anyway, the customs hall was always cluttered up with loads of British people wandering round and round in circles, not knowing where to go. They knew they weren't Dutch and they knew they weren't foreigners – God forbid! So where were they to go?"

In 1992, Britain faces the strange prospect of joining forces with (dare one say fellow?) European nations apparently as intolerant of their own particular minorities as we were of ours. Arabs were vilified by much of France, new ghettoes awaited Turkish Gastarbeiter arriving in West Germany, whilst in Holland, Indonesians formed the ignored and impoverished underclass. Stranger still was the fact that many Australians looked upon us Europeans, in this instance immigrant Italians and Greeks, as wogs. They didn't care much for Poms either. That's me and thee. As Alexei Sayle would say . . . "Funny old world, innit?"

However, racism was not sustained by anything as hysterical as blind hatred or even misguided fear. For most people, common prejudice was perpetuated through an absence of thought, a slip of the tongue. Generic terms such as 'Paki shop' or 'Chinky chippy' were what spread the disease. Whether uttered on television or between bedfellows who knew they meant no harm, these seemingly innocuous phrases would soon become common parlance. That kind of damage would take a lot to undo. It was only right and proper that the nation's youth should go on marches against apartheid or make nuisances of themselves on the pavement outside South Africa House, but if they trotted out, "See you in a couple of minutes, I'm nipping up the Paki shop," every time they ran out of milk or matches, well, the exercise became cosmetic.

But perhaps it wasn't such a bleak picture as one might have imagined. Roland was quite encouraged by the number of FYC fans and the widespread popularity of other multi-racial bands, not to mention reggae groups. He reasoned that . . . "If someone likes a group with black members, then they are far less likely to turn out as a racist bigot." One suspected that Fine Young Cannibals didn't go in for anti-racist dogma because too many well-meaning bands who wore their hearts on their sleeves ended up sounding patronising, sometimes painfully so. What such groups lacked was balance. Fine Young Cannibals fans, however, understood one thing: where other bands shouted, Gift and Friends barely whispered.

Generally, these hints sufficed. Andy, for instance, was an utterly committed, one might even say devout vegetarian, and Roland's 'my body is my temple' kick was as wide as a bus, but such personal ideals were seldom expanded on in interviews and *never* in songs. There was never any militancy, never any evangelism.

Acutely aware of the trendy 'good bloke with heavy socialist leanings' trap, which in the ex-members' opinion The Beat haplessly fell into, FYC opted for a music free from clichés. Any direction that they had was accidental, artistic, not ideological. They were naturals. A live set which placed covers of Elvis Presley's 'Suspicious Minds' and The Buzzcocks' 'Ever Fallen In Love' alongside 'Move To Work', and what was to be the band's second single, 'Blue', showed that performing good songs was their prime consideration. Andy and David had been down the agit-pop road before, so they were wise to the pot-holes.

"We were so credible," said David, recalling The Beat. "Towards the end we were living off our credibility when we should have been doing it with the music. Nobody would slag us off for writing such diabolical songs because we were doing all those benefits. We were supposed to be these good old blokes, you know . . . But let's face it, everybody's more pissed off if their girlfriend leaves them than if there's a right-wing dictatorship, aren't they?"

"We don't want to become one of these so-called political groups," Andy told *Record Mirror*'s Mike Mitchell. "It was never our intention. I'd much rather hear Michael Jackson or Prince than a thousand of these Faith Brother type of earnest young bands."

"People should say what they think," offered Roland, "but I just wonder how many of them actually believe what they say. It's, like, a good way to make your mark. In a lot of cases it's all done with careerist intentions, but you can never really be sure unless you know them. After all, you could say the same about me."

'Blue' was a fine example of a disarmingly commercial tune spiced with a tang of conscience. As with 'Johnny Come Home' the group made more than one attempt at recording the song, again falling back on their neat, original version. Its hook was a galloping chorus endowed with a bite: 'Good God almighty, there's no denying life would be better if I never had to live with you, Blue. It's a colour so cruel . . .' Roland didn't beat about the bush: "It's a song about falling out of love with the Government."

As a result, 'Blue' suffered from a good deal of 'negative promotion'. Despite an opportune November release setting it in pole position for 1985's Christmas rush, the record never took off in the same way that 'Johnny' had. External forces were at work. 'Blue' contained several poignant verses – 'My home town is falling down, I'm mad about that; and the people there don't seem to care, I'm mad about that . . .' – which, in the wake of Handsworth's September riots, seemed all the more ironic. The song could almost have been written about the events in which two people lost their lives and scores of livelihoods were reduced to ashes.

This latest bout of civil disobedience occurred about a mile from where Andy and David lived, in a part of Birmingham called Lozells, bordering on Handsworth proper. Lozells was a run-down city district which at best could offer its newest generation of voters poverty, unemployment, or a brief career in either aggravated burglary or heroin. Having withered long in the shadows of Margaret 'Wanna

Buy A Council House?' Thatcher's economic miracle, it was perhaps inevitable that the people rioted out of sheer frustration. It wasn't as if it hadn't happened before, either in Handsworth or in other British cities. Neither was rioting an exclusively 20th Century phenomenon, which was the impression one got from the *Daily Mail*.

"The worst thing about it was watching the way it was covered in the papers," Andy told *NME*'s Adrian Thrills. "The coverage had nothing to do with what actually went on. Even the supposedly sensible papers didn't really offer any enlightenment. If they can be so wide of the mark over Handsworth, you do tend to wonder about their reports from the other side of the world."

"Their two main theories were that it was fuelled by drugs and anti-Asian feeling," David put in. "Just about the only definite thing you can say is that it wasn't triggered by any of those things. The press made out that the streets were running with blood . . ." A cosmetic cover-up ensued.

Concerned politicians made inspection tours of this blighted inner city area, a sociological post mortem was carried out by the media, and the Government addressed the 'problem' most sympathetically by building a new swimming pool. "They also offered people cheap new roofs – and then practically took their houses apart installing them! People were being woken up by workmen crashing through their ceilings!"

All in all, this was about the worst possible time to put out a record which was critical, however mildly, of H.M. Government. Sensitive to anything of a dissenting nature at the best of times, the media was redoubling its efforts to tone down its output, to remain absolutely impartial. Once the faintly disturbing whiff of political content began to tease producers' censorious nostril hairs, television shows booked on the strength of the Fine Young Cannibals exemplary first single were cancelled without notice. The band wondered in their innocence what all the fuss was about: 'Blue' wouldn't exactly change the world, but then again it wasn't designed to. It was just a song. Nevertheless, the TV executives didn't warm to the sentiments expressed so tenderly by our Roland.

"They're pretty fair lyrics," he told *Sounds*' Dave Henderson. "But these days people seem to be being really cautious. For instance, the BBC's got to be careful: they don't want to put a foot wrong especially when we're building up to an election and we're in the middle of Maggie's image-softening campaign. They don't want anything that's in the slightest way contentious."

"The problem is that it does actually say 'Government' in the lyrics," David went on. "If they had referred to the 'Big Man' or the 'Fat Cats' then it might have been a different story."

Radio, too, behaved in the same fawning manner and it soon became obvious that 'Blue' was receiving only a third of the airplay allotted to 'Johnny Come Home'. Andy and David began to experience feelings of *déjà-vu*. This was a virtual re-run of The Beat's 'no nukes is good nukes' single, 'Stand Down Margaret', a record which was suppressed out of existence on national radio. Its fiercely pro-CND stance meant that most jobsworth disc jockeys were disinclined to play it on their shows. Times hadn't changed much, obviously. A pair of seasoned cynics, Andy and David looked upon this media censorship as inescapable. After all, it was only the BBC exercising their much-vaunted right of reply.

Christmas approached and social issues fell out of the news. In New Zealand, the authorities were searching for French Secret Service agents who sank the Greenpeace flagship 'Rainbow Warrior' in Auckland harbour, whilst on the other side of the world Fine Young Cannibals watched 'Blue' grind to a halt at number 41. A trifle unfair, but not to worry. Andy, Roland and David had an album up their proverbial sleeve, an album of substance with which they were very pleased indeed. "It's got a really pathetic title," beamed David. "It's called 'Fine Young Cannibals'."

With half a dozen windows open on their Advent calendars, Fine Young Cannibals watched their eponymous début LP being snapped up like so many roast chestnuts. In just three short weeks, 'Fine Young Cannibals' achieved gold status, eventually selling in excess of a million copies worldwide. Appropriately, the album received a considerable nod of approval from the music press, praise which had not been lavished on a chart band since The Smiths charmed their way out of the alternative scene and onto Radio One's daytime playlist.

THE SWEET & THE SOUR

Sounds' Dave Henderson noted that these abundant blessings couldn't hold a candle to the proud fathers' own ardour. "It's got to be the best album around," they thrilled, "because everything's right on it. The songs are the best, the trumpet player is the best you can hope to hear all year and even the hi-hat playing is better than anyone else's. The backing singers are better than most lead singers and even the tambourine will take some beating!"

Several critics excused their own wholesale enthusiasm by daring to venture that it was a response to the dearth of lusty opposition on the home front, newcomers seeming more content to reiterate past styles and poses rather than develop any original methods of getting their angst out. There were exceptions, but very few.

The Pogues, for example, were honest, bawdy folk, with a tremendous capacity for rabble-rousing. Though they may have had about as much musical finesse as the All-Ireland Hurley Final, The Pogues put derivative combos like The Mighty Lemon Drops to shame. No one was duped by Echo And The Bunnymen forgeries any more. As for The Housemartins, the less said the better. Strange as it may now sound, all eyes came to rest on over-hyped style renegades Sigue Sigue Sputnik, albeit fleetingly. Salvation was at hand! – or so their advertising men would have had us believe. They were, of course, nothing short of a total embarrassment.

David Steele, the humble man for whom the mighty Martin Degville used to make shirts, registered his disappointment with *Record Mirror*'s Betty Page. "I thought some great noise would come out and overwhelm me," he sighed. "I thought they had to be something really wild but their music's just Euro. I wouldn't mind if it was really terrible, but it's not even that..."

'Fine Young Cannibals' enthralled everyone by delivering the goods. The talent responsible for the preceding couple of singles had been hard at work keeping its promise of high fibre, low-fat pop. Having completed much of the groundwork using a basic eight-track, familiarising themselves with the structure of each individual song and trying out various brass and string parts, it was then possible for the group to upgrade the raw material in a superior recording studio with the minimum of fuss. Consequently, the album was finished in under four weeks, rather than the protracted three-month Bahamian norm. With the exception of the self-produced 'Johnny Come Home' and 'Funny How Love Is', the bulk of the album was produced and mixed with eminently capable assistance from Robin Millar, whose most recent production credits included Sade and Everything But The Girl. Roland in particular held him in high regard.

"Most producers like to put their stamp on a record. You know, have themselves on it rather than the group. But because Robin Millar's so successful he doesn't have to worry so much. There are no ego problems – he just does what's best for the song."

Similarly, expectant Cannibal watchers were greatly taken with Roland's vocal mastery, many referring to him simply as 'The Voice'. "In a business where identity is all," wrote Richard Jackson in *Record Collector*, "he has the advantage of sounding utterly like himself and no one else. Technically more gifted singers would kill for less."

"At present," added *Melody Maker*'s equally impressed Will Smith, "there are few people to challenge Roland Gift's expressive sense of loss. Supposed 'soul' singers might feel compelled to grunt and groan in order to prove themselves, but Roland need command no such cheap theatrics. His voice is instinctively given to communicating the bleak and ugly sense of despair. His ability to sound *hurt* is as remarkable as it is effortless . . ."

Long tracts written about the singer's vocal abilities didn't quite amount to eulogy, but comparisons made between his voice and past soulmasters Al Green, Sam Cooke, Smokey Robinson and, of course, Otis Redding, were hard to ignore. Though the final analogy was perhaps naïve and a shade undiscriminating, the fact that the music press were now bracketing a precocious Roland Gift with one of the world's all-time great vocalists endorsed the popular view that Roland was indeed the Fine Young Cannibals' trump card.

"Obviously it's very flattering," he conceded, modestly. "But I don't let it go to my head. I just know it's better than someone saying I sound like Billy Idol . . . I think people come up with names like Otis Redding because they need some kind of reference point. But he *was* the one who made me want to sing, really want to sing. Listening to him, that was the first I understood about what singing could be. 'That's How Strong My Love Is' still brings tears to my eyes."

Roland was also at pains to point out that he had never contrived to sound like any of the hallowed sixties singers. He was influenced, as we all were, by those people for whom we had more than just a passing regard. Liam Fay of *Hot Press* went one step further by asking if that "big, corrugated voice of his" was natural or affected? "It's just the way I sing," replied Roland. "It's not put on. People are always surprised when they hear me speak because it doesn't sound the same. I don't know why that is."

Roland's favourite track on the LP was 'Couldn't Care More', the first of two ballads which, he maintained, were the album's winning touches. 'Couldn't Care More', with its seductive skipping start, together with the love-battered melancholy of 'Funny How Love Is', made 'Fine Young Cannibals' as complete and impressive a début album as could ever be wished for. This was no soggy assemblage of stale tunes destined to reappear six months later in secondhand stalls or the record store dumper. It was a treasure, pure and simple. An appraisal of Tracy Chapman's equally impressive début album read . . . "For all the vagaries of fashion, old-fashioned values like good songs well sung aren't so old-fashioned after all." Exactly the same could be said of 'Fine Young Cannibals' with its bold, familiar patterns.

The tracks were reminiscent of those once-cherished songs which, when you heard them on the radio, made you turn up the volume and smile. Instrumental subtleties and understated use of backing vocals served to heighten this effect, with only Roland's voice ever being allowed to dominate. Even on pacier tracks like 'Time Isn't Kind' and 'Don't Ask Me To Choose', Andy's guitar was never intrusive. Flavoured by David's classic Hammond/Farfisa organ playing, Graeme Hamilton's lonely trumpet and Saxa's lilting saxophone on 'Funny How Love Is', 'Fine Young Cannibals' had a faint taste of better times gone by. Love and disillusionment were every bit as much the album's hallmarks as its disciplined percussion and moments of instrumental charm. But why, asked *Record Mirror*'s Andy Strike, were the lyrics on the LP so anguished and full of heartache?

"Happy songs are never any good, are they?" offered David. "Unless it's 'Sugar Sugar' or a couple of The Monkees' songs. All the greatest songs ever written have been really sad, except a couple of Motown things. I like emotional, heart-wrenching songs . . . This is about the best my life's ever been at the moment and funnily enough, it's probably the most miserable music we've ever done."

One of Andy and David's strongest motivations during the recording of 'Fine Young Cannibals' was . . . "To wipe away the guilt of the last group we were in, we set out to make at least one LP that would just sound brilliant and last a long time. I think we've succeeded."

'Fine Young Cannibals' went on to spend a total of 25 weeks in the album charts, reaching a high point of 11. With such an impeccable LP to their credit, Fine Young Cannibals finished off 1985 on a note of elated satisfaction. This was something of a quantum leap for a band who had begun the year, like so many young hopefuls, on less than a wing and a prayer.

"The difference between the Fine Young Cannibals and the rich and famous is only a matter of time," wrote Ted Mico in *Melody Maker*. "The Fine Young Cannibals are good, a perfect band for the eighties. Three haircuts with not a follicle out of place. The crops are ready for harvesting with stylish yet anonymous clothes, sophisticated yet elementary tunes, and stirring yet sterling back-beats. They are

THE SWEET & THE SOUR

the bright young things of 1985. Front covers, rave reviews, and bottoms up."

Not only had their music achieved widespread popularity in a relatively short period of time, the Fine Young Cannibals 'look' was fast becoming established, appreciated. The group's image, from their appearance on television, on video or in magazines, to their quasi-constructivist record sleeve grafik, was always clean, ordered, even wholesome. But it was never smooth, never striped shirts and Next silk ties. They abhorred suits and with little hesitation stated that their favourite colour was black. Fine Young Cannibals could never be mistaken for one of those new Aryan office boy groups, all blond hair and City suits, whose videos invariably featured a token *femme fatale* and whose odourless, wine bar pop could no more be cherished than a paper plate. Very professional, but decidedly dull. Too un-American to be 'pop', too quirky to be casual, the Cannibals chose a wholly individual style which reflected their music. Blue and black jeans featured prominently. FYC were, however, trendsetters without acolytes.

"I don't mind if people dress up like us," grinned David. "Although I think they'll have a hard job creating a look that's just a cross between Marks and Spencer and second-hand clothes shops in Rotterdam." To a great extent, the bulk of the band's wardrobe was gleaned from downmarket stalls rather than classy designer-label fashion houses. "I don't like new clothes," Andy told *No.1*'s Debbi Voller. "You pay 10 times too much for them and they just disintegrate. Also, there's nothing worse than wearing in a new item of clothing – old ones have already been worn in for you."

"It's great to wear items of clothing that never go out of fashion," agreed Roland. "But I do hate ironing."

Andy, who was still an habitué of jumble sales, favoured voluminous cardies and trousers full of dead men's farts, fought over and won in time-honoured tradition. Prior to his conversion to more conservative garments, Andy had fallen foul of childhood fads, as had the other two. They all remembered with a kind of fond horror dressing with the flair of a trainspotter. Maroon corduroys or loon pants with three-inch high waistbands were *de rigueur* in the early seventies, as were striped tank tops and platform shoes. Welcome relief came with the demise of Glam Rock and peer pressure shifted in emphasis from uniformity to individuality and then to nonconformity when punk happened along.

"That's when I started going to jumble sales," Andy continued, "and I discovered old fifties clothes that were made out of reasonable materials: good cotton instead of shitty nylons. In the fifties they cared about what things were made of and they paid attention to detail. The shirts, for instance, have good little features like buttoning pockets and clips."

Though not as important as their music, such attention to detail was certainly an integral part of the FYC make-up. A band with an inconsistent or confused image was like a shirt frayed at the cuffs: irritating and uncomfortable. Unlike many bands who took their cue from stylists and designers, Fine Young Cannibals always dressed in an original fashion. Not especially daring or innovative, but of their own creation, and they were satisfied with it. In its essence it was unlikely to change much. "I mean, it's just basic good taste," affirmed David. "We don't wear anything we wouldn't wear when we go out on a Saturday night."

"While David may be kidding about only wearing anything made before 1958 by old Italian gentlemen," observed Graham K. in *The Hit*, "their look *can* be pinned down to a fairly specific period in the early sixties. It ain't mod, though. More an older guy's appreciation of considered cool. It's low-key, tasty, occasionally eccentric in its pairing of checked waistcoats with clashing sox, but never, *ever* flashy. Cut together with essentially brief haircuts and baggy-bum skinny-leg pegs, it doesn't bellow at you but speaks volumes for the group's quiet chic."

Some of the developments arising directly from the impact of their collective appearance took the band by surprise. These included having their photographs featured in Italian *Vogue* and the French fashion magazine *Elle*. They were also asked to do a catwalk show in Paris. Clearly, FYC had begun to make an impression outside of the music world. But had their meteoric rise to prominence actually made them stars? Roland laughed. Fame was still something of a novelty, a fringe benefit that got him and the others invited to a lot of parties.

"I suppose the oddest thing is people coming up to you and asking for your autograph, things like that. Quite often, though, people see me and they think I'm a Roland Gift fan who's dressed up trying to look like me! That's quite funny."

David, for whom autograph hunters were a nightmare come true, told *No.1*'s Kate Davies that he didn't so much dislike being recognised in public, more that he hated the embarrassing situations which arose every now and then. "Like you're in the queue at the fish shop," he squirmed, "and some guy comes up to you and says, 'You're in the Fine Young Cannibals, aren't you?' And everybody else looks at you and they don't know who the hell you are! It's not like some gorgeous chick saying, 'Hi, Davey baby . . .'"

Andy demurred. "We don't want to be famous. Fame is more a by-product of what we really want to do. I don't think we'll ever be as famous as Madonna or Prince. Now *they're* famous!"

SEX, GINSENG AND ROCK 'N' ROLL

Where Fine Young Cannibals failed to capitalise with 'Blue', 'Suspicious Minds' returned them swiftly to the upper reaches of the Top 20. Lifted from an otherwise wholly self-penned album, the band's ever so slightly tongue-in-cheek cover of one of Elvis Presley's last great and truly soulful songs, his last US number one, was a predictable success. Released in January 1986, the record matched 'Johnny Come Home' in rising to number eight, and in common with their first single it too appeared in several gimmicky but collectable guises, not least of which was a seven-inch picture disc. Limited edition, naturally.

Dubious marketing strategies aside, the group's choice of a song from 1969 rather than the King's unimpeachable pre-G.I. days, spoke volumes both for the band's musical sensibilities and their sense of humour. Whilst FYC shared the under-forties' incredulous dismay at the memory of the Las Vegas ham dressed in a rhinestone-studded white leather catsuit, Presley's sad souvenir image, they recognised a good tune when they heard it. Andy, Roland and David had also considered covering Chairman Of The Board's 'Give Me Just A Little More Time' and 'Working On A Building Of Love', but felt that whilst they were perfectly able to do the songs justice, they couldn't really add anything to them. The songs just didn't lend themselves to a genuinely original interpretation.

The idea to revamp 'Suspicious Minds' came, Andy claimed . . . "to David in a dream about Elvis." Taken

THE SWEET & THE SOUR

with a pillar of salt, this suggestion seemed plausible enough. David was, after all, a collector of tacky Presley memorabilia, among whose most prized possessions was a musical box which played 'Hound Dog' whilst a miniature Elvis danced on the top. He also had an amazing capacity for watching crass Carry On Elvis movies well into the small hours. Laudably, the group managed to augment the original version with restrained use of strings, an accentuated middle eight in 6/8 time, and skirling falsetto backing vocals courtesy of Jimmy Somerville, on loan from label-mates Bronski Beat. "We'd heard that we were his favourite band at the time, so we just phoned up and asked him."

Suffice to say, Fine Young Cannibals made 'Suspicious Minds' more complete than The Damned's uninventive yet faithful reproduction of Paul and Barry Ryan's 'Eloise', or Phil Collins' 'You Can't Hurry Love' or Los Lobos' 'La Bamba' or . . . Mark James, the man who composed 'Suspicious Minds', agreed. On hearing Fine Young Cannibals' lively rendition he dashed off a letter to the band saying how much he liked their cover, having heard scores of substandard attempts since Elvis' death in 1977.

'Suspicious Minds' was a further kick in the eye for those who still seemed intent on saddling the forthright Cannibals with the title 'Spokesmen Of A Generation'. Hell, the band wanted to play love songs as much as the next man! And without any snide comments about having sold out, either. What your average Fine Young Cannibal desired, bottom line, was to make good records – for dervishes one day, dreamers the next.

Come the time of their repeat *Top Of The Pops* performance, the group were off and away in the United States. The concerts they gave during this first visit were quiet, showcase affairs, save for one occasion when some bright spark let off a canister of CS gas. Their performance at New York's Ritz club was filmed for broadcasting on MTV. "Mostly they were really good gigs," Roland told *Record Mirror*'s Betty Page. "It was a really good feeling. The reaction surprised me, and so did the people. A lot of them were trendy, which was a surprise because a lot of Americans don't know how to dress. Bjorn Borg came to our New York gig, and Talking Heads came to see us in Los Angeles . . ."

In March 1986 came the turn of France, Belgium and Luxembourg, the band returning home just as 'Suspicious Minds' dipped out of the Top 60. A follow-up single, 'Funny How Love Is', backed with the 'bluesabilly' 'Motherless Child', was released in April. Despite the re-mixed version boasting violins and backing vocals, the record proved far too subtle a flavour for popular consumption and it duly stalled at number 58. Maybe Joe Punter was too busy tooling up for the World Cup to notice such a plaintive love song. Claves? Bongos? A triangle? Leave it out, mate . . . "Here we go! Here we go! Here we go!" *Melody Maker*'s Mick Mercer was on the right track when he gave it five, voting 'Funny How Love Is' his record of the week – 'When at first you left I thought I'd surely die, I couldn't see a future without you by my side; we're not together but I'm still alive, I'd rather

FYC **50**

SEX, GINSENG AND ROCK 'N' ROLL

The recording of 'Funny How Love Is', on which David got to grips with a borrowed double bass, led indirectly to a minor disaster. So taken was Mr Steele with the instrument's acoustic qualities that he thought he'd pop out, dig deep, and buy one. Only in the music shop he was suddenly overcome by a fit of severe mal-coordination and stumbled headlong through the shop's display, completely writing off one instrument. Trapped by his total embarrassment, he was unable to leave the shop without making some kind of conscience purchase.

Meantime, FYC were pushing the boat out once again, giving a total of nine performances in 11 days up and down the country. In Cannibal terms, this April jaunt constituted serious touring, though the string of British dates had taken considerably more effort to organise than the group had originally anticipated. Roland outlined the problem to *Sounds'* Dave Henderson.

"There just aren't any good places that fall between the Hammersmith Odeons of this world and the Wag Clubs," he complained. The difficulty lay in the fact that even at this early stage in their existence ('Johnny' hadn't yet reached his first birthday), Fine Young Cannibals were already a shade too far on the 'mega' side to appear down your local community hall, whilst the group eschewed cavernous Top Rank-style ballrooms on the grounds that they had about as much to do with a good night out as Victor Kiam had to do with subliminal advertising. Cosy yet capacious venues were clearly hard to come by, yet find them they did, and not just in the big urban centres either.

not see you for a very long time.' – How often the misses were mightier than the hits. Certainly, it made a fine album track, but in retrospect the more up-tempo 'Time Isn't Kind' or 'Don't Ask Me To Choose' might have been more logical out-takes. Typically, the band appeared unperturbed by its comparative failure.

THE SWEET & THE SOUR

No.1 correspondent Anna Martin unearthed the band at Chippenham Goldiggers and came away impressed.

"It's a good job the dance floors were built to last!" she enthused. "By the third number the crowd is excitedly heaving, and the once merely catchy 'Blue' becomes something of a sing-a-long as Roland prowls with the effortless style and grace of Frank Bruno – jutting and weaving, slipping and sliding. The rubber legs of Andy Cox jerk uncontrollably, distorting his body in a frenzied attack to match David Steele's equally wobbly movements. Covering almost every inch of the stage between them, FYC skip through songs from their début album, throwing in an unexpected cover of The Buzzcocks classic 'Ever Fallen In Love', as well as Andy Williams' 'Can't Take My Eyes Off You', for maximum appeal. In a word, FYC are stunning."

Suspicious minds? Not a chance. Fine Young Cannibals were on the up and up. Strange, then, that the group should have chosen this particular moment to begin falling out with journalists – usually in restaurants – just as they were beginning to win over the press *en masse*. Their main beef, it transpired, was that the repetitious nature of promotional work, compounded by the pressures of stepping it out lively on stage every evening, was beginning to grind them down. Motorcades of tape machines queued to absorb their daily regurgitations, and even the ever-garrulous Roland began to blanch when he heard someone pipe up with . . . "Where *did* you get that name from?" All in all, expending their energies on such increasingly trivial pursuits made the group very fed up. And when they were fed up, they began to get difficult. Awkward. Uncooperative. Mardy, as they say up north. Or so *Melody Maker*'s Will Smith was warned when he turned up to question them.

"I think we decided yesterday we really don't like doing interviews any more," yawned David. "I think I'd rather become a recluse. It's not like being tortured with electric probes, but we've just got to cut them down a lot. It's unhealthy. Once, we did 22 in one afternoon. And this is, like, the 200th interview we've done in the last two months."

Where before there had been cheerful intercourse, a state of mutual distrust now existed, especially between the three Cannibals and reporters from the 'heavies'. A frivolous question-and-answer session, followed by the obligatory photo session would generally leave them in good humour, but any attempt at an in-depth feature met with increasing caginess. As a result, dissatisfied reporters invariably transcribed their listless conversations in sarcastic tones, the group ever vulnerable to the poison pen. Sympathetically, *Record Mirror*'s Betty Page conceded that the band couldn't be expected to fizz all the time.

Roland: "It's like fat days and thin days."

David: "I don't have that many fat days."

Ms Page: "Please, have a fat minute, just for me. Be a sport."

David: "Well, the interview's going really well so far, isn't it? Got some good stuff here."

Ms Page: "I wanted to get something new and interesting out of you."

David: "I don't think anyone's said anything about us, whether good or bad, that has even any relevance, and it never does. You don't even get a slight

THE SWEET & THE SOUR

impression of what we're really like."

Such dismissiveness soon earned the band a reputation among interviewers for being 'stroppy bastards', a reputation which they loathed every bit as much as yesteryear's trendy leftie tag. They found interviews boring. It was as simple as that. In a characteristic outburst of paranoia, David put down one particularly bad record review in *NME* to the fact that the lads had been somewhat over-zealous in slagging off people who wore leather trousers – thereby unwittingly consigning half of the *NME* staff to the sartorial dustbin. As 1986 progressed, so the ripples in the mill-pond stilled. No new singles were sent scuttling after 'Funny How Love Is' and interviews all but dried up. After a year in the limelight, Fine Young Cannibals were enjoying a well-earned stretch of the legs. For them, this was the intermission.

By Midsummer's Eve, as the Wiltshire Constabulary slung a thin blue cordon round Stonehenge in preparation for the annual New Age hippy bashing festival, the only spoor left by our heroes was a classy little LP retiring gracefully from the album charts. As the group hadn't made any specific plans for the immediate future, Andy and David chose to unwind by taking part in the UK property boom, swapping their red-brick Handsworth terraces for deceptively spacious flats down in London, south of the Thames. The time was now ripe, they thought, to move from beloved Birmingham. As luck would have it, they would still be living close enough together to pop round for a cup of sugar.

During the late seventies and early eighties, London's importance as the music industry's epicentre had waned – albeit briefly – as independent regional labels dared challenge the big guns. Now the trend was reversing, Messrs. Cox, Steele and Gift felt it was essential for all three of them to be closer to the centre of things. Being in London also made it a good deal easier for the band to work together and simplified the everyday business of running a group. Culturally speaking, too, it was vital for the team to be strategically positioned. Compared to a bustling, cosmopolitan city like London, Birmingham was very much a neglected part of the Provinces.

Eagerly the band picked up on the burgeoning club scene, a vibrant source of underground influences as yet untapped. And for the expatriate Brummies, living in the Capital also meant no longer having to wait months to see new films. For a pair of avid film buffs like Andy and David, this was just cause for celebration. David, having fewer sentimental ties with Birmingham than Andy, had no real

SEX, GINSENG AND ROCK 'N' ROLL

qualms about moving to London. He said the city had gone downhill ever since they closed Barbarella's. Andy, on the other hand, was less enthusiastic, at least to begin with. What he missed most about his corner of Birmingham was the close sense of community, from people's warmth and friendliness to the basic feeling that he simply belonged there, that he was part of it. However, the neighbourhood where both he and David now lived was in many ways similar to their old Handsworth home. The area was multi-racial, its buildings had seen better days, and the main thoroughfare inching towards the West End was redolent of Handsworth's own Soho Road. A diversity of food stores, eating places, and specialist travel agencies represented the local ethnic population and a preponderance of carpet remnant warehouses, secondhand shops and off-licences betrayed the fact this, too, was an area of slender means.

For Andy, the most positive aspect of moving to London was that never again would he have to suffer going through customs at Birmingham International airport. The frequency with which both he and David were stopped, sometimes for an hour-and-a-half, followed by a long and wearisome taxi ride home, really had him despairing. Without fail, every time they flew back to England late at night after having appeared on some Continental pop show, they would have to go through the additional performance of being searched for drugs. Pop stars were like that, see. Drugs coming out of their ears. Shocking it was. What sort of answer were you supposed to give when a uniformed customs officer's most tactful opening gambit was, "Do you take drugs?" Either laughter or dismay.

"At least at Heathrow," said Andy, "they have the intelligence to realise that a drugs courier is probably going to look like a business man with a Samsonite briefcase, not some scruffy musician in need of a bath and 15 hours sleep."

THE SWEET & THE SOUR

Before the big move, David recalled that he could scarcely imagine Andy and his wife uprooting themselves from their home. It was so imbued with personality that he had come to regard it as part and parcel of the Andy Cox he knew. But, he reflected, the couple had managed the transition well enough and Andy's assorted collections – cacti, commemorative plates, rocks – were quite settled in their new home. Andy was also the official repository for band memorabilia. Where David kept nothing, apart from Malu Halasa's book on The Beat... "To have a laugh at the pictures every once in a while," Andy hoarded just about everything. From photos to his cherished Japanese FYC pencil case, Andy kept it all. It seemed slightly curious that the shy, public Andy Cox should be FYC's private 'memory man'.

David, always the more relaxed and expansive in company, inhabited rooms with bare floorboards, pictureless walls and few places to park one's behind. Piles of videos, CDs, tapes and records slumped against the TV, and magazines fanned out from every available corner... "I hate shelves," he stormed. Judging by the kitchen, he hated washing up, too. There was no jacuzzi, no swimming pool and no bedroom with ceiling mirrors, though David was proud of having laid his own patio. Quite an engineering feat that. When Fine Young Cannibals weren't working in the studio, David's messy, small-windowed basement was where the group gathered to mull over new ideas or create the basis of new songs. Amid the dormant piles of washing, stacks of books and sundry boxes, there was just about enough room for a small amplifier, beat-box, tinny keyboards, a couple of dull-stringed guitars, and a battered washing machine. A Japanese walnut piano stood against one wall, buried under discarded overcoats and an ironing board stood permanently to attention. The room looked more like an earthquake zone than a hit factory.

When alone, FYC personnel would either watch TV, eat, listen to one of the better pirate radio stations, drink beer or read. Roland was particularly fond of the disconsolate poetry of Ted Hughes and Sylvia Plath, or in fact anything that moved him enough to make him cry. Generally speaking, the group's taste in books was very much like their taste in music: pretty catholic. As reading matter they cited everything from *Viz* comic to *Milan Kundera*, via reference books on Russian post-revolutionary textiles. Nothing unusual. Their TV diet ran mainly to films, current affairs programmes, a good serial like *The Singing Detective* and the odd soap, with an additional bent for anything bizarre, such as sumo wrestling or hands-down-the-trousers late-night talk-shows.

It was not something FYC actively publicised, for obvious reasons of propriety, but the band expressed a great liking for all things camp. Not the

mincing stereotyped ITV gay, but the ambiguity and brazen don't-care attitude of a person wholly at one with their sexuality. Neither were Andy, Roland and David afraid of public displays of affection for one another, an idea which would strike them as completely ridiculous; embraces were common and they often parted company with a kiss on the cheek, a peck on the lips. Roland, for one, loved to give people flowers. They weren't the ones with a hang-up . . .

Although they all lived to eat, the one thing Fine Young Cannibals did disagree on was food. On what was to be eaten they had, uh, irreconcilable differences. Andy never ate meat, though he recently braved some fish in Thailand, and Roland pursued a clean-living macrobiotic diet with the zeal of an ascetic. David, on the other hand, would have wasted away without at least one fried breakfast a week. He was also partial to the occasional cheeseburger. "I think some of the food I eat winds Roland up," laughed David. "The other night I ordered white rice in a restaurant and he was telling me I was going to die of cancer just from this one bowl . . .! But, thank God, Andy's not one of those Nazi vegetarians." Mostly, they ate out . . . "Which is surprising because we've all worked in restaurants. We know that if you complain, somebody will gob in your soup when they take it back to the kitchen. Or they'll stick their fingers in the sauce to taste it. Still, if the record company's paying . . ."

Roland's one weakness was that he liked, or rather needed, to get drunk.

And unlike his friends, he was no connoisseur. This was the darker side of the Gift character. "I go mad now and again," he told *No.1*'s Jaynie Senior. "You see, if you're writing songs and things like that, you need some kind of outlet – you need to rave – just to get it out. Because it gets to you after a while . . . I've got a temper but I've learnt to control it. When I was younger I couldn't. If I wanted to let off steam I'd go out and break a load of milk bottles. One by one against a wall." However, he disciplined himself never to drink on stage just in case he lost control of his voice and went out of pitch, which is every singer's nightmare. So, instead of Andy or David's strategically located cans of beer, Roland refreshed himself with nothing stronger than Adam's Ale.

The Fine Young Cannibals' second and more extensive US tour was as support to the Brumbeat reggae of UB40 during 1986. David and Andy had known them since their pre-Two Tone days, when a stage for the two bands had been little more than the stuffy end of a flock wallpapered lounge bar in West Bromwich. Now they were sharing an elevated platform in a West Coast amphitheatre, playing to captivated audiences of 20,000. Roland was pleased to inform *No.1*'s Mike Hrano that UB40 made good touring companions.

"I mean, we got soundchecks and we got fed," he recalled. "There was no funny business in that respect. Some bands can be right pigs to their support acts."

Likening this round of touring to being homeless, Roland said the band had been . . . "Lost in America. Once you're out there it's like you're cut off from the rest of the world. You wonder what's happening in Britain and you try to get a newspaper every now and again."

On tour, they put up on friends' floors for some of the time. Hotels offered more comfortable sleeping arrangements, but precious little else. Roland also bemoaned the lack of

THE SWEET & THE SOUR

FYC **60**

municipal swimming pools, the absence of which robbed him of his favourite form of exercise and mile after mile of mental relaxation. When asked their opinion of America, the reply was an all-encompassing sigh – "What can I say?" – but Andy did say that he loved the idea of a country which had 24-hour greengrocers. Contrariwise, David mumbled habitually about the frightening level of violence: Philadelphia was not one of his favourite cities . . . "Give me Rome or Madrid any day. The food's better for a start."

When Andy and David headed for home at the end of the tour, Roland remained behind for an enlightening month's holiday in New York. Amid acres of plate glass and aggressive automobiles, he behaved at first like some limey milquetoast, shying from the brashness of it all . . . "But in the end, I got to know New York, and I'd wander around at four o'clock in the morning without worrying. Obviously there are certain places you can't go – and I didn't go to them! – but I did get to feel comfortable about New York, and I made a few friends."

Blissfully ignorant of Fine Young Cannibals' extra-curricular activities, their home audience marked them down as missing in action. The band and news of recent developments didn't surface until March 1987, when promotional duties tied in with their upcoming single, 'Ever Fallen In Love', brought them bright and breezy, straight into a waiting ambush. For virtually a year this fine and promising young band had been out of circulation, doubtless enjoying themselves at everyone's expense and now here they were again glibly pumping *another cover version* way up the charts. The first new material they've produced in 18 months and it's not even *original!* Outrageous, sir . . .! Plainly, the arbiters of the day required a little more application from their subjects.

"Everybody thinks you're not doing anything, that you're being very lazy," complained David. "We didn't want to put out stuff that was crap. There's no point."

Maybe it had been a big mistake for the band not to have put out any records during the latter part of 1986. But they had done it now and that was that. Without being arrogant in any way, they were of the opinion that this entity named Fine Young Cannibals could have simply cobbled together an album's worth of material straight after the first, just to keep their name in lights. And they would have almost certainly cleaned up into the bargain. But they weren't like that. Still, this squall of discontent didn't really do the band or their new single any harm. 'Ever Fallen In Love' – in its five different formats, including cassette single and compact disc just to make sure all the exits were covered – did very nicely, thank you, in reaching number nine in April 1987.

It soon transpired that FYC hadn't been resting on their laurels after all. The group's latest hit was but the first by-product of their recent American sojourn to be unveiled. 'Ever Fallen In Love', The Buzzcocks' tale of wounded romance, had featured in the band's set for a couple of years, but the song was only committed to vinyl as the result of their recent involvement with a film project whilst in the States. Jonathan Demme, director of Talking Heads' *Stop Making Sense*, starring an athletic David Byrne, was putting together another oddball comedy, *Something Wild*. He also ended up directing FYC's 'Ever Fallen In Love' video. Demme wanted to use the song alongside tunes by the likes of American performance artist Laurie Anderson, so the band set about recording a track which in many ways signified the group's *volte-face*. 'Ever Fallen In Love' marked a watershed beyond which the Fine Young Cannibals' sound would never be the same again.

THE SWEET & THE SOUR

Before this departure from FYC's creative norm, Andy, Roland and David had stuck to a familiar, common ground. Only now did they feel fully confident enough to experiment with a new style, a sound radically different from their established soul-based pop. More importantly, it was a style currently in vogue on the club and warehouse scene, a fact which was not entirely lost on FYC. Many were the nights they spent twisting their heels and spinning their hips to these attractive new beats. Hip-hop had been fighting for recognition for several years, but apart from a few obvious rap and scratch hits, it gained relatively little airplay. Equally, music writers treated the phenomenon as some kind of undisciplined aberration. Not that they were above attaching themselves to the crowds of curious tourists in Covent Garden who gathered to marvel at the improbable movements of body-poppers and robot dancers. A new musical creed was abroad, and its knock-on effects were dynamic.

Meanwhile, FYC continued to dance and drink and watch and listen. A decade ago, legions of deadbeat punks had trashed the old musical order. In the words of the song, they had just strapped on their guitars and played some rock 'n' roll. Now there was a new revolution taking place, a technological revolution. Years of industrious bodywork in Rock's Great Garage resulted in an explosion of hip-hop gangs and house masters who set about rewriting the rules of popular music completely. Punk had had a fair crack at burying the 'boring old fart' rock establishment under an avalanche of brute force, using the familiar tools of guitar, bass, drums and vocals.

In contrast, exponents of hip-hop reduced music – maybe dismantled would be a more accurate term – to its constituent components of rhythm and sound. Using microchip technology common to every High Street in the Western Hemisphere – synthesisers, samplers, record and tape decks, digital sequencers, drum machines and microphones – they rebuilt music to their own design. Sound was welded to sound, rhythm against rhythm, fragments of a thousand 12-inch singles protruded everywhere, and its ugly, erotic form was sprayed from top to bottom with slogans, words and symbols. This was music as it had never been treated before: man and machine in perfect harmony. For the first time in history, music had become truly industrialised. Move over Kraftwerk, here comes the 21st Century! And the function of this extreme noise terror? To make us dance. Prince Charles would never approve of this angular modern music or its architects, but the *restructuring* process was already well under way. Like it or not, it was here for the duration.

What FYC liked about hip-hop and house was its unadulterated energy, its momentum. Like punk it was homemade, born of the street, and for all its apparent multi-layered complexity, it was essentially very simple. S-Express hit number one with a record put together for a mere £800. Unfortunately, the style was open to wholesale abuse. Everybody wanted a piece of the action and the indiscriminate pressing of buttons made anything possible. David was not joking when he said, in his inimitable deadpan slur, that he was thinking of sampling the whistle on his kettle. On the face of it, making music had never been easier. But these machines, while easy to operate, were extremely difficult to master. In insensitive hands, synths and sequencers were capable of creating as much havoc as the sorcerer's wand in the hands of an unschooled apprentice. The medium of video suffered in much the same way: discipline, skill and a critical eye made for good films, not the ability to point a camera in the right direction. Selectivity was the golden key.

Highly attuned to this radical shift in the sound of music, Fine Young Cannibals embraced its less unpredictable elements, picked up their guitars and rejoined the race. David likened music fashion to a moving train, saying that as time progressed and trends had changed from punk to ska to rap and hip-hop, the fashionable continued to ride that train. Those who alighted, who still sported pork pie hats, or had petrol-coloured hair and listened to The Cure, were destined to be shunted up some weed-clogged siding or broken down for scrap. Fine Young Cannibals' recording of 'Ever Fallen In Love' was no token gesture, no mere flirtation. It was a calculated experiment which worked and worked well.

"We wanted to do something unusual," Roland told *NME*'s Stuart Maconie. "We wanted to attempt a cover version that people wouldn't associate with our style and do it in an unorthodox way, as we did with 'Suspicious Minds'. In fact it's backfired, because with all the profit he'll get from it, it means that Pete Shelley won't be forced to reform The Buzzcocks. That might have been . . . a laugh."

A couple of years on, Pete Shelley, the man with the perpetual cold, did exactly that. Much to their fans' delight and the chagrin of the press. 'Ever Fallen In Love' appalled punk purists, those myriad folk who'd flung themselves off David's funky train when New Order released 'Blue Monday'. True, FYC's cover version lacked The Buzzcocks' enchanting abrasiveness, but live the band had long since made it their own. A cool backing track and Roland's easy vocal changed the song's impact completely and criticism about it being some pale imitation seemed unfounded, a misinterpretation of the band's motives. Fine Young Cannibals, like Siouxsie And The Banshees, enjoyed covering old favourites and always did it well. Moreover, Andy, Roland and David were all big Buzzcocks fans, albeit half a lifetime ago.

For all the fuss arising from the release of 'Ever Fallen In Love', it was ironic that in the end the track hardly figured in *Something Wild:* "About 45 seconds," they griped.

The band met with an entirely different reception with their second film venture. Naturally, they had welcomed Demme's invitation, but this unexpected sideways step in their careers was only consolidated when they were approached by Barry Levinson, the director of *Diner*. Levinson had just finished shooting a new movie, *Tin Men*, about aluminium salesmen in Baltimore, starring diminutive funny-man Danny De Vito and Richard *Close Encounters* Dreyfuss. All that remained was for Levinson to dovetail the edited footage with a compatible soundtrack – a soundtrack which would have to

reflect the film's early sixties atmosphere – and the film would be finished. It so happened that songs from 'Fine Young Cannibals', an album which often graced the Levinson turntable, complemented the footage perfectly. But rather than take the easy option of using existing material, he approached the three musicians and asked them to score original music for the film. The group were delighted.

They flew out to Los Angeles to fulfil their commission, whereupon Levinson brought them down to earth by giving them a cramped six-week deadline. "We thought that was kind of unreasonable," Roland told *No.1*'s Mike Hrano, "but we managed. It was interesting to work under pressure." The tracks they recorded were 'Good Thing', 'As Hard As It Is', 'Tell Me What' and 'Social Security'. In a couple of scenes, the group even made a cameo appearance as a soul band, playing their sixties pastiches in the tin men's bar. "You could only see my nose," sulked David.

Roland recalled the experience as being more like shooting a pop video than serious acting. No less a devotee of the cinema than his two companions, Roland described *Tin Men* to *NME*'s Alan Jackson as . . . "a *life* film. It's very funny in parts, very sad in others. Just like life. It reminds me a lot of those sixties English films, like *The Loneliness Of The Long Distance Runner*. It's truthful, which is nice."

As a project, composing a film score had come right out of the blue. As an absorbing sideline, their brief encounter with the film world whetted appetites and, as fate decreed, opened up brave new vistas for the trio. Even rock stars could have lucky breaks it seemed. With Andy and David keeping a close eye on the dials, they went on to score music for *Trains, Planes And Automobiles* . . . "But only because Steve Martin was in it." 'Don't Ask Me To

SEX, GINSENG AND ROCK 'N' ROLL

Choose' featured "on the radio" in *Letter To Brezhnev*, but that didn't really count.

The biggest departure from their lives as musicians was undoubtedly Roland's precipitous move into acting. By-passing the more usual "Yes, Milady" walk-on roles, Roland landed himself a major part in a small British production. Stephen Frears, whose credits included the excellent *My Beautiful Laundrette*, a film scripted by Salman Rushdie's writer friend Hanif Kureshi, took a sudden shine to young Mr Gift when he saw him on *Top Of The Pops*. His 'screen test' in *Tin Men* hadn't done him any harm either. Roland's chiselled features and swarthy physique were the perfect combination for a character in his new venture, *Sammy And Rosie Get Laid*. He got the job.

Described by Channel Four's right-on film critics as "a searing indictment of Thatcherite Britain," *Sammy And Rosie Get Laid* generally received an indifferent response, save for obvious anatomical references following the six-in-a-bed scenes. Roland, who was forever being reminded of the film's heavy sexual bias, met any improper questions with an obstructive smirk, toying with his earlobe or a teaspoon until the conversation changed direction. He preferred to regard the part he played as something of a personal milestone, though Roland did voice certain misgivings at jumping in at the deep end. He believed that should he have turned in a lousy performance as Danny, then perhaps Andy and David's names might have been dragged into the critical mire along with his own. As it happened, *Sammy And Rosie Get Laid*, abbreviated to plain *Sammy And Rosie* across the Atlantic so as not to offend local sensibilities, impressed a sufficient number of directors and casting coaches that he was subsequently swamped with scripts. If there were any parts that Roland *didn't* turn down, he was keeping the matter very close to his chest. Rumours ricocheted off his serene smile like pebbles off a policeman's helmet. As ever, we would just have to wait and see.

LIONS AFTER SLUMBER

Come October time, the Great Leveller visited upon southeast England first a hurricane then Black Monday's Stock Market crash. Not a good day for the yuppies. As for Andy Cox, Roland Gift and David Steele, 1987 was drawing to a close with Fine Young Cannibals having once again dropped out of the frame. In anticipation of the music press's traditional Christmas Dishonours List, more disparaging observers were busily pencilling in the dynamic trio as one-hit wonders.

In retrospect 1987 was no more the band's year than 1986 had been. So, when Messrs Steele and Cox began 1988 on *Top Of The Pops sans* Roland, performing under the banner of Two Men, A Drum Machine And A Trumpet, well, there was much wagging of tongues. As a disembodied voice punctuated their scatty tune, with . . . 'Tired of gettin' pushed around,' whispers began to drift down from the gallery. Had the Fine Young Cannibals divided into two rival camps? Was it true that the musicians had parted company with their singer because he was reportedly too busy pursuing an acting career? And was it more than coincidence that Andy and David lived practically next door to one another, while poor Roland was left to inhabit some lonely north London outpost a dozen miles away? The rumourmongers put two and two together and, as ever, came up with 15.

The truth of the matter proved simple enough. Some time back in 1987, whilst Roland was on sabbatical, Andy

THE SWEET & THE SOUR

and David were told by their record company that they had to come up with a B-side for their proposed new single – at that time 'Good Thing' – and quick. With Roland unavailable, the pair booked into a studio and set about tinkering with whatever sounds and equipment came to hand. This was the first and only time that FYC had composed away from home. The 'house' tracks with which they soon emerged – 'Tired Of Getting Pushed Around' and 'Make It Funky' – were an acknowledgement of their off-duty nightclubbing. Confident that their mix matched up to what they were hearing around town, Andy and David hatched a plan to have 'Tired Of Getting Pushed Around' released in its own right.

This was towards the end of 1987, when only a few giveaway titles – Krush's 'House Arrest', Yazz And The Plastic Population's 'Doctor In The House' – had successfully staked a claim for the flourishing acid house underground in the national charts. As per usual, nobody showed anything more than a passing interest in this new craze and FYC's patrons, London Records, were no exception. They were quite prepared to allow the efforts of the Two Young Cannibals to gather dust. David took up the story.

"Eventually, we put out 'Tired Of Getting Pushed Around' as a white label under the name of Two Men, A Drum Machine And A Trumpet. It was an experiment. We used a pseudonym because we didn't want people to associate it with FYC and if it bombed, well, no harm done. Anyway, once it was played by all the club DJs, it went straight to the top of the Club Chart, the Dance Chart ... After that, London decided to adopt it."

1988 arrived, the year of the dance floor revolution, and here were Fine Young Cannibals' anchormen on the nation's premier pop prog doing what came naturally. In January their record achieved a modest placing of number 18 *with* Roland's blessing. "That song gave us a kick up the backside as well," remarked David to *Record Mirror*'s Steve Masters, "because the Fine Young Cannibals were becoming too middle of the road. It told us not to do covers all our life – like Showaddywaddy."

Over the next 18 months, as Roland blossomed into a fully-fledged celebrity, the question of internal friction and petty jealousies over the group's vocalist moonlighting as a film star would raise its doubting head over and over again.

"I don't think people believe it when we say that we don't mind Roland's acting," David told *Rolling Stone* correspondent Steve Pond. "They really believe it bothers us. But I don't see why we would be upset, really. Why should we mind? If we were sitting at home getting bored, then maybe we'd mind a bit ... It sounds phoney, doesn't it – 'Oh, we don't mind.' It's like, 'We all treat animals really well,' or, 'We have great family lives'."

Roland was quick to echo these sentiments ... "It isn't a problem. I don't think either of them has any acting ambitions and they don't like the idea of being frontmen. At the moment, they're more interested in production work and producers are always reclusive figures."

Even after such unequivocal statements as these, the band could sense a grandstand of reporters craning their necks to detect the first signs of strain, aching for the cracks to appear. The newshounds (not Kennel Club registered) would have loved nothing better than a bit of public bitchiness, a bit of a scene. Or better still, a scandal. Far from sitting at home getting bored, Andy and David were becoming absorbed in their new-found roles as pop producers. Having recently produced 'Tired Of Getting Pushed Around' and assisted in the production of virtually all Fine Young Cannibals material, the pair soon found their knob-twiddling talents in demand elsewhere. They received invitations from the all-girl rapping crew Wee Papa Girl Rappers, and Pop Will Eat Itself, whom they described as . . . "Mad. The only decent alternative band around."

When asked if the latter group were produced for the vast sums of cash involved, they burst out laughing. "Love!" they exclaimed. But make no mistake, a record producer's fees are attractive, at least to the layman. The advance for an album track was, on average, £1500, rising to around £8000 – that's £50,000 per LP plus a royalty in some cases – for a real wizard, a 'name'. Small wonder that American college courses in sound engineering were massively over-subscribed. As production work was likely to become their main occupation when Fine Young Cannibals called it a day, both Andy and David could feel safe in the knowledge that they might just be able to eke a living out of it. "Besides," they said, "if we do have to work, we'd rather work in a studio than anywhere else."

Did they have any definite plans for retirement? "Depends," mused David. "If we split up next year, I think I'd get another band together. If we split up in five years time, I'd probably do nothing for ages and then start getting restless . . . I can't speak for Andy or Roland."

Top of the group's unrealised ambitions list was really a kind of school-day regret. With all the travelling they did, they wished that they'd all studied languages. As for basic get up and go, Roland told *NME*'s Jim Shelley that he was very ambitious . . . "Like a *demon*. I don't know why. It's like this character that inhabits my body. It's constantly there but sometimes it just fills me, just to remind me. Just to say: 'don't forget, you bastard, you've got something to do'!"

David laughed at the idea. "I don't have any ambition at all! But I wouldn't mind having a small tattoo done of Felix the Cat."

"And I'll have one of Googie Withers in an eagle's talons," said Andy drily.

Behind the mirth and the mixing desk, Cox and Steele operated as a team . . . "Just as we've got identical

THE SWEET & THE SOUR

tastes in music, we usually have the same ideas about how a record should sound. There's never any time wasted through disagreement. The re-mixes that we do are essentially for our own enjoyment." Fine tuning was Andy's job. He was, conceded David, not only the partnership's but the group's superior musical technician: "He's better at marrying soundtracks to film than I am, and at programming sequencers." Both favoured the same equipment, usually obscure relics dating back to the sixties, and they constantly bemoaned the fact that there were few mixing desks around that gave the warm sound they had grown so fond of over the years. Distance was no object, all that mattered was The Desk!

And the people they were being asked to produce . . . Professional, and with a bent for perfection, they were left feeling mightily guilty when one session with Pop Will Eat Itself was . . . "Completely cocked up." David added rather sheepishly that he and Andy decided against having themselves credited on that particular release. They had substantially greater success with Wee Papa Girl Rappers, whose single 'Heat It Up' made the Top 10. Appearing amid 1988's deluge of hip-hop, rap and acid house acts, the main criticism levelled at Wee Papa Girl Rappers was that they were, sin of sins, commercial.

Their producers, however, had a different viewpoint. "They're such sweet, sweet girls," they said with almost paternal concern. "I know people call them commercial, but anything that gets them out of boring lives in north London high rises has got to be good."

One of the more curious side-effects of production work, which the pair had in fact been dabbling in for nigh on 10 years, was that David had developed a compulsion for checking and double-checking things. Before leaving his flat he would go through the ritual of making sure that all the electrical sockets were made safe, that the windows were locked, the back door bolted, and the gas cooker turned off. Half way down the road, he would sometimes be compelled to turn back just to make absolutely sure that nothing had been left on. Much to his girlfriend's annoyance. What with Andy's alleged fridge and suitcase phobias, Roland's undisguised fear of both heights and flying, and David's additional fears of his person being attacked or blown up in an aeroplane, FYC seemed riddled with enough neuroses to warrant a case history in six leatherbound volumes.

The root of David's mildly obsessive behaviour, from which Andy appeared to be quite immune, was Mixing Desk Psychosis: an early-hours light-headedness caused by constantly monitoring dozens of recording levels and concentrating on countless other minute details through hours, sometimes days, at the controls. A couple of FYC tracks had demanded 36 unbroken hours' work before a satisfactory mix was arrived at. 'Good Thing', for example, in which the sounds and responses were different to most pop records, with very little snare or bass, just handclaps, had apparently been a right pig. Now just remember next time you're dancing to it, a lot of love, sweat and effort went into those sweet three minutes.

Meanwhile, 1988 was idling slowly by and the group's record company were wondering aloud when they might deign to produce their crucial, long-awaited, make-or-break second LP. Not that the band had any contractual Sword of Damocles dangling over their collective head, but it was noted in high places that more than two years had passed since the appearance of 'Fine Young Cannibals'. As spring turned to Summer Of Love (Ecstasymix) and the globe warmed to the Acid House Effect, so the number of telephone calls from their record company increased accordingly.

"We're working on it," came FYC's not so reassuring reply. Actually, much of their valuable time was spent attending a goodly number of Home Counties raves. Solid gone!

Notoriously unprolific – "In an exceptional month we might come up with three new songs" – Andy, Roland and David had it in mind to include certain of the tracks they had recorded for *Tin Men* on their mythical new album, although plans hadn't progressed much further than that. The telephone calls persisted. Which producer would they like to work with? They conferred. "Um . . . Dunno. Sod it . . . How about Prince . . . ?" They laughed and hung up. Hearts skipped a beat in the London Records boardroom as their boys' suggestion was taken in earnest. More phone calls were made, this time to newly-hip Minneapolis, and the record company's accounts department experienced a shrinking of the fiscal scrotum. Peacocks did not dine on peanuts. The threesome, who would be risking nothing if such a venture were ever to come off, had another cup of tea and thought no more about it . . . Sorry, guys, came the unexpected reply. Prince loves you, but he's going to have to take a rain-check on this one. Would you settle for his second in command, David Z?

Without further ado, Roland, Andy and David packed their bags and made for Prince's Paisley Park Studios, hoping that they might just bump into one of the few contemporary artists they all admired. If they did meet the man – swoon! – it would be, of course, by accident. None of them would ever dream of actually *approaching* him. Alas, there were only brief, breathless encounters, as *Hot Press* writer Liam Fay found out.

"We nodded to Prince a couple of times," recalled Roland jovially. "I think he really does inhabit a different planet from the rest of us. But David Z was great. He was very straight, a really nice person. He invited us to his house and we met his parents and kids and had a barbecue. He was just a normal kinda guy. A bit like us really."

During their stay at Paisley Park, David Z worked on just two songs, 'I'm Not Satisfied' and 'She Drives Me Crazy'. "It was really only one-and-a-half songs: we recorded a new vocal for 'I'm Not Satisfied' back in England." As technicians, Andy and David appreciated Prince's generosity in allowing them to use his customised mixing desk. They were also greatly impressed with Paisley Park as a working environment . . . "Apart from being totally purple inside and designed to make full use of natural light, which is unusual, it's got the best video games in the world . . .! Actually, I think they were all really pleased with us at Paisley Park: 'She Drives Me Crazy' was the studio's first number one."

Working in fits and starts, it had taken the group nearly two years to put their second album together. Its title, 'The Raw And The Cooked', was lifted from Claude Levi-Strauss' book on anthropology, a copy of which lay buried in David's back room. But with characteristic perversity, the band were disinclined to leak the album's name much in advance of its official February 1989 release date; everyone would know soon enough. Roland sometimes alluded to it in interviews, describing the respective sides of the new LP as 'raw' and 'cooked', at which he would smile one of his enigmatic smiles and lapse into silence. Mum's the word, eh? Once under wraps, all that now remained was for the group to oversee the new album's artwork. However, post-production presented the threesome with far more problems than one might have supposed.

Although both Roland and Andy were not averse to exercising their powers of veto, giving final approval of sleeve design proofs, like viewing video rushes, was essentially David's department. The office of group art director was his by virtue of his being the more visually attuned of the three and endowed with keen critical abilities. He appreciated dynamic graphics, and imaginative photography especially, but admitted to finding design work a good deal harder than summoning a tune out of a piano or playing bass.

"Life would be a whole lot easier if we just let the record company design the sleeves," said David. "And have them tell us exactly what to do in videos – and in the recording studio, come to that! – which is what most groups do. That's why 99 per cent of bands have such terrible videos and terrible artwork. Funnily enough, we had more artistic control on Go Feet than we do with London. It's only because we work so hard that our artwork comes out looking how we want it to look."

He also said that designers, as well as their designs, required almost constant supervision. But not for the reason that they were bereft of an understanding of the band's desires. Far from it. It was more a question of making sure that the record company didn't meddle too much with the layout. As the company were the ones who picked up the tab, this tended to be a frequent occurrence and 'The Raw And The Cooked' was no different in this respect. Unanimous applause greeted the outer sleeve, dominated by a striking pink FYC logo boldly underscored by a cuddly group montage, but there was much disagreement over the record's inner sleeve.

Already crowded with codified credits, London's executives were determined to include 'pack shots', neat little pictures advertising the Cannibals' back catalogue. The group took a very dim view of this and the long-suffering design team found themselves caught in the crossfire. In the end, the company bosses won. But only because they cheated. The group were out of the country when the final design was approved, so the inner sleeve was on its way back from the printers before Andy, Roland and David could voice any further objections. Chalk up another one to experience.

Shrewd businessmen by anyone's standards, the band couldn't always be on their guard. "In this game," they grumbled, "not only do you have to be a semi-skilled lawyer and a part-qualified accountant, it helps if you've got eyes in the back of your head as well!"

They lost a second battle when the powers that be insisted on including 'Ever Fallen In Love' on 'The Raw And The Cooked'. The group didn't feel that it was a 'filler', more a case of the song being a bit of an anomaly, like 'Tired Of Getting Pushed Around'. Still, they weren't in a position to argue. "We didn't want to include it on the album," said Roland. "But the record company insisted and there wasn't really a lot we could do. I mean, they've been pretty good up till now. They haven't given us much grief over the fact that it's been a long time since the first album, so we had to capitulate."

THE SWEET & THE SOUR

Towards the dog end of 1988, Fine Young Cannibals were once again ready to face the music. Or in David and Andy's case, as ready as they would ever be. In accordance with the band's unwritten work roster, it was now Roland's turn to do his bit – "He's our sex symbol and adman," quipped Andy. Much in the way that kids and lazy husbands left their mums and wives to do the washing, cooking and ironing, so Andy and David were glad to leave the PR chores to Roland. Besides, he was infinitely more diplomatic than the other two and therefore less likely to put anyone's nose out of joint. Roland's only misdemeanour was a Cheshire Cat habit of excusing himself mid-interview "to make a phone call" and disappearing with a grin into thin air. But on the whole he embraced the task with sickening freshness, announcing to all and sundry that it was . . . "great to be a pop star again!"

"Basically," said David, by way of an apology, "Andy and I are just anti-social. We don't like being nice and pally just because we have to, not that we're into intimidating people or being obnoxious for the sake of it. It's just that when you've got a stinking hang-over and someone asks you, 'Do you enjoy touring?' for the ten thousandth time, well, you're just not going to be that interested, are you? Nobody believes us when we say we don't care what people write about us, but we don't. Really."

It sounded corny when they said it, but only the music was important, making good songs and finding the perfect beat . . . "That, and doing the artwork and the videos, I suppose." If it was known that an interviewer was intent on making a bee-line for Roland, Andy and David wouldn't bother turning up. Why should they waste their already overstretched resources being ignored? Similarly, the three musicians no longer agreed to every possible photo-opportunity. Prospective photographers were asked to submit portfolios and if the men in black liked what they saw, then they obliged. This was happening less and less often: "*Rolling Stone* and the big fashion magazines have good photographers, but the ones from the music press are the pits. Generally, if someone's doing a feature on us, we send along the best of what we've got on file . . ."

LIONS AFTER SLUMBER

It wasn't that the band weren't excited, or that they were trying to be amazingly cool about unleashing a wonderful second album on an unsuspecting world. Rather that their own particular high had come several months earlier as 'The Raw And The Cooked' finally took shape. By comparison, worldwide marketing of FYC product and the requisite high profile neither thrilled nor fazed them. They walked past gigantic posters of themselves pasted on boarded up shopfronts as if they weren't there. Dazzling window displays, videos on TV, phone-ins, radio quizzes: it was all part of the big sell, part of their job. Only this time it nearly got out of hand.

There followed a period of several months during which Fine Young Cannibals, purveyors of modern soul-pop, were totally transformed into FYC, the unstoppable music machine. In the same way, "Isn't that Roland Gift?" was suddenly elevated to . . . "Roland, *darling*." Roland, darling, soon had his work cut out to keep pace with the pressures of fame. On a work day he would rise at six am, to the admiration and horror of his more nocturnally inclined workmates, for interviews and yet more interviews. These were sometimes conducted at his members-only private club, Groucho's, in Islington. Andy and David usually made it in time for a late lunch. Discounting Roland's real estate investment, a modest 4,000 acre hedge against inflation in New Zealand, membership of Groucho's was probably his biggest indulgence. He didn't own a Rolex watch or drive a Porsche. In fact, neither he nor his fellow travellers could so much as drive. One ambition they all shared was the desire to pass their driving test – as distant a goal to the Fine Young Cannibals as making hit records was to the man in the street. Or his car. Until such time as Roland was able to set aside a couple of uninterrupted months in which to learn this basic 20th Century skill, he was happy to continue being ferried hither and thither by taxi . . . "'Ere, you'll never guess who I had in the back of my cab the other day . . ."

Holding Court in his club's pleasant surroundings, with its plush armchairs and bowls of olives, Roland was on home territory. The exclusive club had cowed many journalists in its time and intruded upon many an interview, but Roland enjoyed its friendliness, its *privacy*. Membership was, perhaps, to be expected of a *face* like Mr Gift, whom *NME*'s Stuart Maconie described as . . . "The face of the late eighties. Black, affluent, stylish; whether glancing suavely from the screens of the new, sexy British cinema or enigmatically on the glossy covers of lifestyle magazines and twelve-inch singles. Something about him is coolly emblematic of our times."

Yet not for one moment had Roland squandered his ideals in the face of voguish yuppie excess. Quite the contrary. It was not unknown for him to chomp at the bit about being . . . "The only black face in the audience at the theatre last night." Or to rave contentiously about Meibion Glyndwr being champions of the homeless. Their arson campaign may have given off an acrid stench of nationalism, but burning Welsh cottages was apparently all right by Roland.

"They should do it in Scotland as well," he told *Time Out*'s Isabel Appio. "There's something funny about people owning lots of houses. I don't need much space. I've developed a small gait, like people in prison . . ." To Roland's way of thinking, no one had the right to own a second home and leave it unoccupied, whilst runaways were forced to sleep rough, gravitating towards dubious havens like Cardboard City. Formerly situated amid the concrete splendour of Festival Hall and the Hayward Gallery until the authorities saw fit to block it off, this makeshift sanctuary had since moved to its present location in the Bull Ring, right in the heart of Southern Region commuterland, a few yards closer to the Mother of Parliaments. But still downwind, O! Lucky Ma'am. The sentimental Ralph McTell image of eccentric, wandering winos was long gone; there were new, young faces around the burning ring. To tackle Roland on the issue of homelessness was to invite his righteous indignation, a passion expressed most eloquently in 'Johnny Come Home'. It was ironic that the homeless situation in Britain was much worse now than when the song first came out.

In 1989, both FYC and The Stone Roses took Britain by storm. As one journalistic wit put it, the latter's flares were . . . "Three feet wide and rising." Across the ocean, 1989 belonged solely to Andy, Roland and David. As your Chinese horoscope would have informed you, this was The Year Of The Fine Young Cannibals. In January, FYC put their best foot forward, releasing 'She Drives Me Crazy'. It was an absolute stunner and near enough as perfect as a pop song could be. Sexy, fast and beautiful, its callisthenic beat kept us warm and dancing through the long winter weekends. On workdays and weekdays, too, the rhythmic whipping of 'She Drives Me Crazy' was inescapable. Wherever you went – in pubs, in cafés and in City wine bars, hairdressers, night clubs and especially on the car radio – it hogged the limelight, brashly elbowing everything else into the orchestra pit.

The song's introduction was a classic piece of rock bombast, with Andy doing exactly what he had vowed he would never resort to, crashing out fistfuls of power-chords as if to herald the band's return. You could almost hear Thin Lizzy's Phil Lynott thrashing on his harp, humming approvingly, 'The boys are back in town . . .'

Some had not relished the wait. *Record Mirror*'s Steve Masters commented wryly . . . "An original song by the Fine Young Cannibals is about as rare as a four-leaf clover or a straight banana. There aren't many of them about, but it's exciting when you find one."

And there was that Roland Gift chappie again on *Top Of The Pops*, all love and laughter. Boy, was he enjoying himself! With arms outstretched he made as if to embrace both the cameraman and the nation, his frail mayfly voice swelling to the song's full-throated refrain. As an advert for 'The Raw And The Cooked', 'She Drives Me Crazy' said it all. Catchy melody, precise, economic arrangement, and sherbet dab lyrics. Alternatively, from the pen of a thoroughly gratified Stuart Maconie came . . . "No pompous burbling about Belfast, no bastard bagpipes and no penny whistles." Released unto a nation primed by their Top Five single, 'The Raw And The Cooked' took a firm grip on the album charts on both sides of the Atlantic and didn't look like letting go a full year later. FYC had arrived at the hard hybrid sound of the nineties: universal success was assured. Elegant, intelligent, 'The Raw And The Cooked' was eulogised to death and its sales reversed Britain's trade deficit overnight.

Seriously though, by the end of 1989 the album had grossed more than the annual gross domestic product of some Third World countries. Think about it. An average of around 20,000 copies crossed the counter worldwide every day. Seven million is quite a big number. The band were flabbergasted, Roland especially. "I've never seen seven million anything," he told Mat Snow in *Q* magazine. "Seven million nails or seven million Smarties, I wouldn't know what it looked like. I don't know what it means. You don't know who's buying them or why."

Roland's singing, which on the album ranged from wafer thin ('Don't Let It Get You Down') to a rich molasses ('As Hard As It Is'), was again carried shoulder high through the streets. Earlier comparisons with 'the greats' were made anew, yet depending on how he used his voice, Roland's lyrics were intelligible only when it suited. On 'Don't Let It Get You Down', for example, the intensity of his words – 'There's a club I can't get in, every week it's the same damn thing, I get mad, I want to cry: is it my skin they don't like?' – was partly obscured by technique. There was no desire to be completely up-front, a charmer. With no lyric sheet to accompany the album, FYC's music still possessed more secretive corners.

THE SWEET & THE SOUR

The only trace of a backlash came from those cynical sourpusses who claimed that both the album's hi-tech sheen and its state-of-the-art sound had been wrought by producer David Z. The fact that the sparse 'Prince funk' was currently very popular – as aped by INXS on 'Need You Tonight' – seemed to have passed them by completely. Again, Roland soon put the record straight. "David Z's contribution was crucial but limited," he stressed. "He was only actually responsible for a couple of tracks. We had the songs.

Though the album may sound extremely modern, all the stuff can be played on an acoustic guitar if need be. So it isn't just a studio trick. There are strong songs there."

"I think London made too much of the Paisley Park connection," added David. "They were probably trying to get a little extra publicity for the album. We made it all over the place." Similar criticism came forth once it became known that madcap Jools Holland performed the improvised piano solo on 'Good Thing'. Everybody suddenly took it into their heads that he was responsible for each and every ivory tickled on 'The Raw And The Cooked'. Admittedly, David wasn't up to such nimble-fingered pyrotechnics, but he found it particularly galling to have all his keyboard playing dismissed out of hand . . . "I mean, who writes the tunes?"

When the band were recording 'Good Thing' they knew that a *bona fide* piano break would be the cherry on the proverbial cake. Having heard Jools Holland play on The The's recent album, they picked up the phone and asked if the maestro would oblige. They hadn't expected it to backfire so. FYC were not bimbos. The indie school of thought – those who clung desperately to The Jesus And Mary Chain, and various imported weirdos like The Sugarcubes and The Pixies – placed the band all too conveniently in pop's empty-headed, uncreative commercial zone. Whilst they performed in the same arena, Fine Young Cannibals' music was about as far from Stock Aitken and Waterman's beefcake-luvs-cheesecake teen-beat as was conceivably imaginable. We should be so lucky.

"I know what they do is very popular," said Roland. "But so are Wonderloaf and cigarettes – and they're bad for you." To FYC, the whole of the alternative scene was just plain dead and irrelevant. FYC kicked sand in the face of those wimps! Though Roland would probably apologise for it afterwards, Andy and David certainly wouldn't. So what if trendy people with car phones bought their CD's or checkout girls danced round their handbags to their music? This was one of David's favourite themes.

"We reject the Alarm Roadie look," he ranted. "We reject the Smiths-are-God theory, the indie-equals-credibility idea. To us it's just a joke."

"I think people have got it into their heads that we're much more contrived than we really are," said Roland. "Perhaps that's understandable because these days every band is a marketing exercise . . . People make records these days, not songs."

Some bright unattributable spark labelled FYC's rockin' funk as 'designer pop', the word 'designer' having lately ingratiated itself on any acceptably clean germ-free surface. But the label seemed somehow irrelevant outside of London's yuppie enclaves. Driving round Clapham Common brought out David's yobbishness . . . "Excellent pubs. Shame about the yuppies."

"I know what they mean by 'designer pop'," said Roland. "But as criticism it's a wide ball, it's way off the mark and I'm going to stay in my crease and refuse to play it."

NME's Stuart Maconie seemed well pleased: "Roland's lack of animation is a joy to behold. He clearly couldn't give a shit whether FYC are regarded as a

THE SWEET & THE SOUR

major contrivance or the last word in cool."

The Cannibals' cause, and more especially Roland's acting career, were further advanced when *Scandal* went on general release. By the time 'Good Thing' reached the number seven slot in April, everybody was talking about this brand new British-made full-length feature film about the Profumo Affair. Roland's face was everywhere. After he was interviewed on Breakfast Television, someone was quick to christen him a . . . "multi-media hot potato."

Scandal relived the Government-toppling events of 1963, when Cabinet minister John Profumo's reputation was put through the shredder as revelations about his personal life – bedding 'call-girl' Christine Keeler – appeared in the national press. His big mistake, however, was to have compromised our dearly beloved National Security, something which still gives the Government apoplexies today. You wouldn't win any prizes for turning up at a 10 Downing Street Fancy Dress Party dressed as Peter Wright. Sex scandals, by comparison, were somewhat passé and not worth disrupting a ministerial post for. Paragon of virtue Cecil Parkinson would doubtless second this.

The central character in *Scandal*, played by John Hurt, was Stephen Ward, the scapegoat who had introduced Christine Keeler not only to John Profumo but to a Russian embassy attaché as well. Pillow-talk, you see. Dangerous talk costs lives and all that. Suffice to say, when the story broke in the same year that Beatlemania first hit the headlines, at a time when public outrage knew no bounds, the events which unfolded in Court viz Stephen Ward living off immoral earnings and the linking of John Profumo's name to this 'prostitute' eventually precipitated the downfall of the MacMillan government. Phew! The whole can of worms only came to light after another of Christine Keeler's lovers, an unsavoury character by the name of Johnny Edgecombe, took a dozen or so potshots at Ward's mews apartment where she lived. Which was where our Roland came in. The part of Keeler's 'bit of rough' was played by his handsomeness, Roland Gift, complete with ultra-violence and diluted patois.

"Johnny's an interesting character," he told *Melody Maker*'s Dean Haynes. "It's a smaller role than *Sammy And Rosie*, but Johnny's an important character. You couldn't tell the story without him. It was one of the most interesting roles I've been offered. I wanted to do something that was worth doing rather than something I'd be embarrassed about. Something good. The story in *Scandal* is something that was of great historical importance at the time. All the people involved were practically household names; it was such a big issue."

The film's importance was that skeletons were now coming out of the cupboard, just as America's collective guilt about Watergate had to some extent been purged in films like *All The President's Men*. But, we were told, *Scandal* was not the *whole* story. The spectre of national security in the form of MI5, plus vested interests of detachable heads higher up, meant that certain aspects would be hushed up for a long time to come.

LIONS AFTER SLUMBER

Roland told *Hot Press*'s Liam Fay that he saw this restriction of information as verging on the sinister. Great Britain was hardly on a par with Albania but the Government *were* loathe to tell you what they put in the water, what went into cattle feed, where toxic waste was dumped, why there were leukaemia clusters around nuclear power stations . . .

"It's indicative of the way things are going in England at the moment. There is a definite repression of free speech and access to information. And now you have a situation where someone like Elvis Costello is banned from live television because he slags off Margaret Thatcher. It's very sad and very sickening."

Make no mistake, though their music had turned into a more commercial enterprise, politics was still uppermost in the FYC mind. Later in the year, as thousands of Chinese students were massacred in Tianenmen Square, David described it as . . . "The death of Socialism. Well, Communism, at any rate." They were moved to witness the end of the Berlin Wall and the emancipation of the Warsaw Pact countries. Historical times these. 1989's world events were a greater talking point within the band than their album reaching number one on both sides of the Atlantic.

Scandal, which also starred the beautiful Joanne Whalley-Kilmer, was not the year's only film about sixties British folklore. Neither was it the only film to feature a rock star. *Buster*, in which fellow pop personality Phil Collins was cast in the title role, concerned itself controversially with the Great Train Robbery. As actors, both suffered the inevitable criticism of being pop stars 'dabbling' in film, a crossover with which neither music nor movie critics ever seemed to approve. This was in spite of creditable performances by Deborah Harry in *Union City*, Art Garfunkel in *Bad Timing*, Roger Daltrey's *McVicar* and Tom Waits as the Motorcycle Boy's alcoholic father in *Rumblefish*. Then again, watching Tom Conti act circles round David Bowie in *Merry Christmas Mr Lawrence*, it was perhaps understandable. And maybe Sidney Poitier couldn't sing.

"I think Frank Sinatra and Doris Day combined the two pretty successfully," commented Roland. "The British have a real problem with this. Their attitude is much less healthy than elsewhere. It's rubbish. Life is much more interesting if you have varied interests. And I don't say that as someone living in Fairyland. I think it is a workable ethic to live your life for everyone."

The post-Cliff Richard vogue for putting singers in films was initiated by Nicholas Roeg. He directed Mick Jagger in *Performance* and a young David Bowie in *The Man Who Fell To Earth*, though neither was really required to act out of character. Jagger played a shaggy-haired has-been rock star who had sunk into a life of sex, drugs and self-indulgence, while David Bowie acted gaunt, weird and vulnerable. Therefore, Roland's portrayal of a real-life "hot-headed psychopath" was a much greater test of acting ability. Unfortunately, his performance earned little praise from Johnny Edgecombe the man . . . "Yes, I heard he'd complained about the way I depicted him, but look at it objectively. He goes around carving people up and blowing holes in doors to make a point. Now I don't know about you, but I regard that as fairly extreme behaviour. I did my research."

The prospect of further interference from one of the personalities involved in the original scandal was the least likeable aspect of its filming. Roland heard that some were putting heavy pressure on the actors to have themselves portrayed in a certain way. As for shooting the film . . . "I just wandered in, did my bit and wandered out again. Three days rehearsal, two days filming and one morning's photo session."

Roland's appearance in *Scandal* brought forth more acting opportunities, ranging from the sublime to the ridiculous. The most bizarre part to come his way was that of a Rastafarian in ITV's cuddly community cop programme, *The Bill*, for which he was told he would have to 'wear' dreadlocks. "My agent said, 'Don't be ridiculous. He won't do it. And anyway, he doesn't have dreadlocks.' And they said, 'Oh well, we can always stick some on him.' That's the weirdest script I've been offered to date."

Twice he has turned down parts in *Miami Vice,* and at one point there were rumours that for a tidy two million he was to play Che Guevara opposite Meryl Streep's Eva Peron in Oliver *Salvador* Stone's screen adaptation of the musical *Evita*. Instead, Roland said he planned to go on the road for six months with the Hull Truck Theatre Company, who were touring with *Romeo And Juliet*. "Well, what would you rather do? Shakespeare or Andrew Lloyd Webber?"

If he put on some weight, Roland might do equally well in *Othello* . . . "It would be nice to do some live theatre again because it's so completely different from film and I really do like live work. I prefer singing live to laying down audio tracks in a studio. I find it more inspiring."

Roland's standing in America owed very little to his appearance in *Scandal*. In the States he was a pop star full stop. And a sexy one at that. From young girls to gay guys, they all came after Roland. "I do use my looks, I suppose," he told Mat Snow in *Q*, "because I do work in pop and film, theatre and that. And a lot of that is your physical appearance and presence. But you don't get off on it. It could be a problem if I felt I *had* to be sexy. If we had been as successful as this five years ago, it would have been harder to handle. I like the way I look, but I don't think I'm in love with my image."

Fine Young Cannibals enjoyed unprecedented success virtually all year in the United States. 'She Drives Me Crazy' went to number one, as did 'Good Thing'. 'The Raw And The Cooked' dislodged Madonna's 'Like A Prayer' from the top of the album chart and remained there for most of the summer. It sold two million copies in less than six months. Only two acts in the entire universe shifted more units than FYC, Bobby Brown and Guns N' Roses, whose frontman Axl Rose adored these freaky-looking London boys. Up in Canada the album out-sold everything for more than five months. David marvelled at the fact that per capita the Canadian population owned more copies of 'The Raw And The Cooked' than any other country in the world. Yup. No doubt about it, FYC were Enormous. With a capital E. Sick-making, wasn't it? When the royalties began to percolate through a short time from now, Andy, Roland and David would be very wealthy young men.

"We've made so much money, it's a joke," Andy told *NME*'s Jim Shelley. "Everybody said at the start, 'This shit is hot, man,' but none of us were prepared for this at all."

THE SWEET & THE SOUR

"The first impression I got of how big we were," said David, "was when the 6,000 tickets in New York went on sale and they got 58,000 calls in one day. Then I thought, 'It's not a hype'." Roland tut-tutted. He was more prudish on the subject of money. Typically, he threw up a smokescreen: "There's more to life than making money, going out with models and driving a BMW. I'm more interested in collecting skills than possessions."

The reasons for their success remained a mystery, to the group as much as anyone else. Their first LP, 'Fine Young Cannibals', had only been a modest hit in America, despite 'Johnny Come Home' and 'Suspicious Minds' having featured heavily on MTV. So what unseen hand had transformed these erstwhile barrow-boys of pop into international mega-stars? In themselves they didn't *feel* any different. The only explanations appeared to be cynical ones, that FYC had taken what the Americans loved best – R&B, soul, funk, hip-hop – rolled it into a tight curved ball and had given it the ol' Babe Ruth treatment. Andy's answer was more straightforward. "It must be our turn," he said to *Rolling Stone*'s Steve Pond. "Every year there's one British group that does well in America, isn't there? You pull the handle, and this year it's three lemons and us."

"The funny thing," added David, "is that Americans get so excited about us when De La Soul should be on the cover of *Time* magazine. Because their LP was so far ahead of anything else."

Obviously, the group's image was a dominant factor. On video they were all hard looks in minimal surroundings. Two skinny white guys sporting exaggeratedly cropped haircuts, the kind that fell from grace along with Lyndon B. Johnson, and a handsome, feline black guy – it had a lot more clout in the States than at home. Ironically, few people in Britain gave their vaguely *American* image a second glance, whilst in America itself FYC's dressed-down streetwise look spoke of British rock 'n' roll vagabondage. This tied in neatly with the band's patronage by the US underground scene where they were referred to as a college band, a term usually applied to the likes of Joy Division, The Fall, Echo And The Bunnymen, The Cure, New Order and, until recently, REM, and which might be loosely translated as 'indie' in the UK. But for Fine Young Cannibals to be played alongside names like these *and at the same time* figure prominently on the black urban dance scene, that was something else. The two camps were poles apart and for the Cannibals to have cross-fertilized, as it were, was of no small significance.

They, along with the likes of Neneh Cherry and Soul II Soul, were regarded as part of a welcome British 'soul invasion', something which had never happened before. Small wonder the band couldn't get a handle on any of this. There was a feeling of subversiveness about it all, a kind of weird excitement. "Imagine if The Stone Roses had a number one album in Britain," said David. "And The Inspiral Carpets or The House Of Love or whoever were at the top of the singles chart at the same time. That's how it's looked upon for us to be where we are in America. It's a really big deal over there."

Despite the offices of the band's US management playing host to tens of thousands of FYC fan letters, the band had no plans as yet to launch a fan club. They felt a slight pang of guilt at leaving this mountain unanswered, but there simply wasn't the time available for such an offshoot to get off the ground. Andy and David had devoted a lot of energy into helping run The Beat's fan club, so they knew how much work would be involved. The size of their following was overwhelming, to say the least.

To confound them even further, Andy, Roland and David were offered several lucrative advertising deals, including giants Pepsi and Coca-Cola, none of which were simply dismissed out of hand. Carefully they examined the merits of each individual campaign, but nothing lived up to David's ultimate accolade of 'cute'. The usual beer 'n' cigs ads were rejected for being sexist; a Spanish perfume called 'Valerie' was thrown out when they heard tell it was tested on laboratory animals; and they turned down Honda because the idea of seeing themselves doing a rerun of the 'Good Thing' video on tinny scooters struck them as horrendously 'tacky'. They weren't about to blow their well-earned respect for a fat fee and an even cushier lifestyle. Maybe when they were past it . . .

The band also cared enough to ban their own records from going on sale in South Africa. Black market discs were available, but these had been smuggled across the border from Zimbabwe of all places.

In August 1989, 'The Raw And The Cooked' spawned its third, though not quite so devastating hit, 'Don't Look Back'. Just how many more were they thinking of lifting off the LP? "Four! Five! Six! All of them!" laughed David, spinning round the room. "They're all brilliant!" Donning their red and green 3-D specs, Fine Young Cannibals fans perused their prized twelve-inch versions of 'Don't Look Back'.

Meanwhile, Andy, Roland and David sneaked quietly out of the back door, with a well-rehearsed umpteen-piece band in tow and embarked upon a projected four-week tour of America and Canada. But they proved to be even more popular than Freddy 'the Fingernails' Kruger so that it wasn't until the end of October that the entourage eventually returned home, more than a month overdue and totally amazed at their reception . . .

"The kids loved us everywhere," they said in a half-embarrassed, shell-shocked voice. One of the few countries which had not yet succumbed to FYC hysteria was Japan, where the band could barely muster a cult underground following. Needless to say, they didn't understand that either. Still, Fine Young Cannibals' promised appearance at America's Grammy Award ceremony in 1990 ought to rectify the matter: Japan's population was included in the 800,000,000 viewers estimated to watch this rockbiz gala via satellite. And Japan always followed America's lead . . .

Special guests and honorary band members on the 1989 US tour were The Mint Juleps, an all-girl acappella group native to London's East End. These five Cockney lasses, with whom the Fine Young Cannibals first became acquainted when they asked them to do the backing vocals on a TV show,

THE SWEET & THE SOUR

David fondly described as ... "the crudest girls I have ever met." There was a mixture of shock and terror in his voice when he said it. Unfortunately their second guest, Neneh Cherry, a former vocalist with those crazy avant-garde scat-cats Rip Rig And Panic, collapsed on stage during her second performance. She was later diagnosed as having contracted Lime's Disease, a debilitating virus carried by deer tics, an epidemic of which was sweeping America's eastern seaboard.

"It's a good job she came down with it in the States, because they know the symptoms over there. If she'd have developed it back in England, none of the doctors would have had the faintest idea what was wrong with her. It can be pretty serious."

Her replacement, for a total of seven gigs, was De La Soul. They opted out after taking a vote on whether to continue with the tour or not. The vote went two to one against. The 10-week jaunt took Fine Young Cannibals from east coast to west, between which a hundred radio stations with call-signs like anti-AIDS drugs never let up playing their songs, and Roland checked into almost every hotel under the rather suggestive assumed name of Leroy Saveloy. Below the Mason-Dixon line, they played to audiences the first five rows of which were made up almost entirely of the promoter's family and friends. The 'thirtysomething' crowd were much in evidence wherever they went and in Los Angeles FYC came bang up against Hollywood. Things began to get unreal. The longer the list of celebrities grew, the more meaningless the names became. Lauren Bacall and Jody Foster had turned out to see them in New York, but now they were well and truly surrounded. Andy reportedly turned down a slap-up feed over at Jack Nicholson's gaff in favour of a cheese sandwich and some TV in his hotel room. You have to laugh.

However, the three of them did keep a dinner date with Madonna and Warren Beatty, organised by the band's management. Like everything else that came the Cannibals' way, they seemed to take it in their stride. They had to be laid-back or else they'd just snap.

"Warren Beatty at the head of the table," said Andy flatly. "Madonna in the middle and us three. It's a different meal from what you'd have in Birmingham, really."

Rather than disband their victorious team of musicians when they arrived back in the autumnal drizzle, FYC graciously arranged a fortnight's sprint around the UK. They opened with a brief residency at The Academy, Brixton, and on three consecutive nights the seatless auditorium was jammed to capacity. One ought to remember that FYC hadn't been seen in the flesh in over three years. Beer at The Academy was grossly over-priced, but this minor inconvenience was a world away for the girls who hugged and slapped the immense pillars adjacent to the stage. Jason Donovan was there, but the girls weren't there to see him. Every vantage point was taken. The music journalists were out in force, too. And not just those from *Sounds* and *NME* either. Scan the arts pages of the *Daily Telegraph* and the *Financial Times* the following day and there were the FYC reviews. A mite fusty perhaps – they didn't pick up the show's humour or love – but they gave the Fine Young

THE SWEET & THE SOUR

Cannibals circus the thumbs up.

As the PA's sounded out the carnival theme from Hitchcock's *The Birds*, the band filed on stage and took up their positions. With Roland under the spotlight, the audience were about to be treated to a bit of honest-to-goodness showbiz. His delivery was theatrical, athletic, comical, especially an hilarious James Stewart running against the wind routine to 'Like A Stranger', straight out of *It's A Wonderful Life*. Roland also gave a brief Jerry Lee Lewis tribute during 'Good Thing' as he ushered Graeme Hamilton out of the way and proceeded to play the piano solo first with his toes, then his bottom. That's entertainment. The Mint Juleps exchanged smiles, instruments and their positions on the stage. They were, dare one say it, underdressed and overweight. Not Prince's Vanity 6. Rubber-legged, Andy and David did what came naturally and behind drummer Martin Parry thrown shapes and the FYC insignia alternated to the rhythms of some of the catchiest pop songs to have whispered sweet nothings in your ears in recent times.

Choreography was tongue-in-cheek for the favourites – 'I'm Not Satisfied' saw Roland and The Mint Juleps galloping back and forth during the chorus – and at its most effective in 'Funny How Love Is'. For this, Roland borrowed Billy Fury's crooning stool, whilst the musicians sat in a line in the semi-darkness like kids on a school wall, picking at guitars or shaking maracas. The appearance of the whole ensemble was casual, light-hearted, at odds with FYC's considered record sleeve and video image. As for the crowd, they were hooked by the rhythms but focusing on Roland's prowling sexual presence as he implored, beseeched, pleaded with the front five rows, holding out his hand.

Throughout the brief 'keep 'em wanting' set, couples were holding hands or hugging each other. Those who had enough room bobbed up and down in time to the music. Afterwards, the questions asked by the group were not, "What did you think of us?" but, curiously, "What did you think of the audience?" Well, there wasn't a single dye-hair in the house – now that surely was a sign o' the times – just happy ordinary folk. "Good," they said. "We were afraid the crowd might be full of yuppies."

What came across so strongly from the Fine Young Cannibals' live performances was their total lack of pretension, the lack of distance between the audience and these famous young men. Outdressed by the crowd, they never once lapsed into anything approaching an arrogant pop star strut; there was nothing in their demeanour to indicate that they were at the top of their league. Roland had a big personality, he was warm-hearted and welcoming, but there were no come-ons, no games, no hosepipes down the trousers. Simply . . . "The people love me and I love the people."

The UK tour went well, they said, save for the Bournemouth gig. They apologised wholeheartedly for the hall's dreadful acoustics. And still their work continued. Andy and David were scheduled to produce Monie Love in February 1990, prior to which they would be promoting 'Good Thing' in France, 'I'm Not Satisfied' in Spain and 'I'm Not The Man I Used To Be', with its melancholy Chapel of Rest organ, everywhere else. With the hours that they were asked to work, they had a lot in common with junior hospital doctors. Dutifully, the band appeared on *Top Of The Pops* but they were furious at the way they and their guests, a five-strong New York City dance posse, were treated by "those upper-middle class twats at the BBC."

"These dancers had flown over especially to appear on the show," raged David, "and the producer wouldn't let more than three of them on that piddling little stage with us. And they went and gave the biggest stage to Tina Turner! Her musicians don't exactly move around a lot, do they?" Evidently, fame didn't always mean better treatment. Not that the famous weren't above misbehaving. On an Italian TV show, sixties relic Joe Cocker, or so they heard tell, was going to sing a pro-George Bush song. While it was being transmitted, Roland and David sneaked up behind the stage backdrop and started lobbing peanuts over the top. There was an uproar and a chase and a scuffle, but they escaped without the threatened broken limbs.

This sort of thing was never planned, it just happened. As with most things FYC turned their hand to, there was no grand masterplan, no worrying about what would come next. And they would never give in to pressure. "People think we're being funny or awkward, but all we're being is true to ourselves," David informed *Rolling Stone*'s Steve Pond. "When groups start out, they have a certain attitude: 'Fuck it all. Bollocks.' And as they get more into the business, they lose that. They think, 'Oh, my gosh, it's an important TV show, we gotta act proper.' We try to keep that attitude – but it's getting harder to keep it, because there's more to lose."

Definitive eighties achievers, Fine Young Cannibals entered the uncharted 1990's keenly aware of both their comfortable rank and the music industry's ceaseless demands. But they didn't lose any sleep over it. They had learned to say no. No to manipulation, no to dodgy offers and no to becoming overexposed public property. Instead, Andy, Roland and David concerned themselves with the details: how they projected themselves and how they were perceived. Above all, they concerned themselves with the music.

The music. What about the music? "I'm not promising anything," said Roland. "That would be foolish. Let's just say you'll always be able to tell it's us. Always."

DISCOGRAPHY

SINGLES

Johnny Come Home/Good Times And Bad
London LON 68 May 1985

Johnny Come Home/Good Times And Bad
London LONP 68 (picture disc) May 1985

Johnny Come Home (remix)/Good Times And Bad
London LONX 68 (12-inch) May 1985

Blue/Wade In The Water
London LON 79 (early copies with 1986 calendar) October 1985

Blue/Wade In The Water
London LONDP 79 (double pack single with free 45 containing Blue (Misery Goat version)/Love For Sale October 1985

Blue (remix)/Blue (seven-inch version)/Wade In The Water
London LONX 79 (12-inch) October 1985

Suspicious Minds/Prick Up Your Ears
London LON 82 January 1986

Suspicious Minds/Prick Up Your Ears
London LONP 82 (picture disc) January 1986

Suspicious Minds/Suspicious Minds (live)/Time Isn't Kind (live)/Prick Up Your Ears
London LONX 82 (12-inch) January 1986

Suspicious Minds (US remix)/Suspicious Minds (Shakedown mix)/Suspicious Minds (live)
London LONXE 82 (12-inch) February 1986

Funny How Love Is/Motherless Child
London LON 88 March 1986

THE SWEET & THE SOUR

Funny How Love Is/Motherless Child
London LONP 88 (picture disc) March 1986

Funny How Love Is/Motherless Child/Johnny Come Home (live)
London LONX 88 (12-inch) March 1986

Ever Fallen In Love/Couldn't Care More
London LON 121 March 1987

Ever Fallen In Love/Ever Fallen In Love (dub mix)/Couldn't Care More
London LONX 121 (12-inch) March 1987

Ever Fallen In Love/Ever Fallen In Love (club senseless mix)/Blue (live)
London LONC 121 (cassette single) March 1987

Ever Fallen In Love/Ever Fallen In Love (club senseless mix)/Blue (live)
London 886 115–2 (CD single) March 1987

Ever Fallen In Love (club senseless mix)/Ever Fallen In Love (rare groove bootleg mix)/Couldn't Care More
London LONXE 121 (12-inch) April 1987

She Drives Me Crazy/Pull The Sucker Off
London LON 199 January 1989

She Drives Me Crazy/Pull The Sucker Off
London LONT 199 (packaged in tin box) January 1989

She Drives Me Crazy (David Z mix)/Pull The Sucker Off
London LONX 199 (12-inch) January 1989

She Drives Me Crazy (remix)/She Drives Me Crazy (seven-inch)/Pull The Sucker Off
London 886 361–2 (CD single) January 1989

She Drives Me Crazy (Manie Love remix)/She Drives Me Crazy (edit)/Pull The Sucker Off
London LONXE 199 (12-inch) January 1989

Good Thing/Social Security
London LON 218 April 1989

Good Thing/Social Security
London LONB 218 (numbered edition in tin box) April 1989

Good Thing/Social Security
London LONT 218 (10-inch) April 1989

Good Thing (nothing like the single mix)/Good Thing (seven-inch)/Good Thing (instrumental)
London LONX 218 (12-inch) April 1989

Good Thing (remix)/Good Thing (seven-inch)/She Drives Me Crazy (Manie Love remix)/Social Security
London LONCD 218 April 1989

DISCOGRAPHY

Don't Look Back/You Never Know
London LON 220 August 1989

Don't Look Back/You Never Know
London LONCS 220 (cassette single) August 1989

Don't Look Back/You Never Know
London LONT 220 (packaged in tin box) August 1989

Don't Look Back (remix)/You Never Know/Don't Look Back (seven-inch)
London LONX 220 (12-inch) August 1989

Don't Look Back (remix)/You Never Know/Don't Look Back (seven-inch)
London LONX3D (packaged in 3D sleeve with 3D specs) August 1989

Don't Look Back (special remix)/Don't Look Back (seven-inch)/Don't Look Back (instrumental)
London LONXG 220 (12-inch) August 1989

I'm Not The Man I Used To Be/Mother's Child
London LON 244 November 1989

I'm Not The Man I Used To Be/Mother's Child
London LONCS 244 (cassette single) November 1989

I'm Not The Man I Used To Be/Mother's Child
London LONT 244 (packaged in tin box) November 1989

I'm Not The Man I Used To Be (remix)/I'm Not The Man I Used To Be (seven-inch)/Mother's Child
London LONX 244 (12-inch) November 1989

I'm Not The Man I Used To Be (remix)/I'm Not The Man I Used To Be (seven-inch)/Mother's Child
London LONCD 244 (CD single November 1989

THE SWEET & THE SOUR

ALBUMS

Fine Young Cannibals

Johnny Come Home/Couldn't Care More/Don't Ask Me To Choose/ Funny How Love Is/Suspicious Minds/Blue/Move To Work/On A Promise/Time Isn't Kind/Like A Stranger
London LONLP 16 (CD: London LON 828 004–2) January 1986

The Raw And The Cooked

She Drives Me Crazy/Good Thing/I'm Not The Man I Used To Be/I'm Not Satisfied/Tell Me What/Don't Look Back/It's OK (It's Alright)/ Don't Let It Get You Down/As Hard As It Is/Ever Fallen In Love
London LONLP 828 0691 January 1989

Red, Hot And Blue

(Compilation L.P. includes 'Love For Sale' by
The Fine Young Cannibals).
Chrysalis CHR1799 November 1990

TWO MEN AND A DRUM MACHINE SINGLES

I'm Tired Of Getting Pushed Around/Make It Funky
London LON 141 January 1988

I'm Tired Of Getting Pushed Around (remix)/Make It Funky
London LONX 141 (12-inch) January 1988